HORRIBLE SCIENCE

FRIGHTENING LIGHT

NICK ARNOLD

illustrated by
TONY DE SAULLES

SCHOLASTIC

Scholastic Children's Books,
Euston House, 24 Eversholt Street
London NW1 1DB, UK

A division of Scholastic Ltd
London ~ New York ~ Toronto ~ Sydney ~ Auckland
Mexico City ~ New Delhi ~ Hong Kong

First published in the UK by Scholastic Ltd, 1999
This edition published 2009

Text copyright © Nick Arnold, 1999
Illustrations copyright © Tony De Saulles, 1999

ISBN 978 1407 10611 3

Printed and bound by CPI Bookmarque, Croydon

10 9 8 7 6 5 4 3 2

The right of Nick Arnold and Tony De Saulles to be identified as the author and
illustrator of this work respectively has been asserted by them in accordance
with the Copyright, Designs and Patents Act, 1988.

CONTENTS

Introduction 5

Seeing the light 8

Horribly bright scientists 22

Bulging eyeballs 42

Sizzling sunshine 56

Frightening lighting 73

Frightening reflections 90

Frightening light-benders 107

Crucial colours 122

Blistering lasers 140

A brighter future? 152

Nick Arnold has been writing stories and books since he was a youngster, but never dreamt he'd find fame writing about frightening light. His research involved tripping up in the dark, staring down the wrong end of telescopes and trying on spectacles and he enjoyed every minute of it.

When he's not delving into Horrible Science, he spends his spare time teaching adults in a college. His hobbies include eating pizza, riding his bike and thinking up corny jokes (though not all at the same time).

Tony De Saulles picked up his crayons when he was still in nappies and has been doodling ever since. He takes Horrible Science very seriously and even agreed to draw an eclipse as it happened. Unfortunately, he couldn't find his crayons in the dark.

When he's not out with his sketchpad, Tony likes to write poetry and play squash, though he hasn't written any poetry about squash yet.

INTRODUCTION

Science is frightening. Frighteningly confusing.

Take the topic of light. You see light every day in sunshine and light bulbs so you might think that the science of light would be light work.

But you'd be wrong. It's hard. Harder to crack than a dried pea from last term's school dinner. And as for the facts – they're harder to untangle than a vat of spaghetti.

See what I mean? Light = instant confusion! It's frightening. And if you ask a scientist to explain about light it's even worse. You're bound to get a long incomprehensible answer with lots of frighteningly complicated scientific words...

Horrible, isn't it? Yep – it's not surprising that Science can make your flesh creep.

Well, now to look on the bright side – here's a little light relief for you. Simply take this book to a quiet place, sit down and turn the pages. It will shed light on light science, and there are lots of light-hearted facts about eyeballs and laser surgery and ghostly lights and other dark and horrible corners of science. These could really brighten your day – especially when you frighten your teacher with a few tricky questions...

Your new-found knowledge of light science is sure to put your teacher in the shade. And afterwards, who knows? You might even become a leading light in science – then you'll really enjoy the limelight! So now there's only one question...

Are you bright enough to read on?

SEEING THE LIGHT

The sun was sinking behind the Brocken Mountain. The sky was getting darker by the minute and already the climber could scarcely see the narrow twisting goat-path at his feet. The climber was beginning to feel very afraid.

"It's time," he thought. "I'm going to see it any minute," and he peered anxiously at his pocket watch.

"Pull yourself together!" he said to himself. "You're a scientist. There must be a rational explanation. There's no such thing as ghosts."

But he trembled and his mouth felt dry as he wondered for the first time how he would find his way down in the dark. A bead of cold sweat trickled down his neck.

Suddenly his heart started thudding. Tiny hairs prickled on the back of his neck.

Somehow he knew even without a backward glance that he was not alone. There was someone ... or something on the mountain behind him. He tried to turn his head but his neck had locked rigid. At last he forced his whole body to swing round. His jaw dropped open in horror. Behind him, etched on the foggy clouds was a huge dark figure. Rings of ghostly light played around the terrifying outline as it hung in thin air.

The thing seemed to be watching him. Waiting. Waiting to pounce.

For a moment the climber seemed hypnotized. Then he forced himself to react. With trembling hands he pulled out a pocket book and a chewed stub of pencil. And started scribbling unreadable notes. All the time he was mumbling desperately.

"Fascinating phenomenon," he said, over and over again. "Fascinating. I – er – better get moving."

As the climber turned and scurried up the path the giant figure seemed to spring into life. It began climbing silently and effortlessly in the climber's footsteps. And whatever it was, it was coming after him, silently – faster and faster.

And reaching out its long shadowy arms...

DON'T PANIC! As the scientist realized, the figure was only his own shadow. This very real if ghostly effect is called the spectre of the Brocken after the Brocken Mountain in Germany where it's often seen. If you climb a mountain near sunset (not a very safe thing to do – so don't try it on your own) the low sun can cast your shadow on nearby clouds. And you see a huge ghostly figure. But this is just one of many horribly amazing light effects.

Read on for the frightening facts...

Frightening light fact file

NAME: Light

THE BASIC FACTS: Light comes from the sun and from hot glowing objects such as candle flames. Oh, so you knew that already? Well get this...

THE FRIGHTENING DETAILS: Some types of light don't involve heat. They include eerie glowing creatures and chemicals that shine in the dark.

(For more info, flick off the light switch and turn to page 73.)

A GLOOMY THOUGHT

So you really did switch out the lights just then? Well, put them back on and read this.

It's easy to make light appear and disappear, isn't it? Every morning light appears in the sky and you don't even have to get out of bed to make it happen. So maybe that's why people take light for granted. And think it's no big deal.

Well, it is.

Imagine the sun doesn't rise tomorrow. Then imagine that all the light bulbs in the world go *phfutt* at the same instant.

And imagine also that even the distant stars fail to shine. The world would be very cold and very dark. And frightening and dangerous. Without light to see by, people would be bumping into each other and treading on the cat and knocking over priceless ornaments and skidding on banana skins.

And that's not all. Can you work out which other things you need light for?

FRIGHTENING LIGHT QUIZ

Without sunlight you can't see...
1 A rainbow. TRUE/FALSE
2 The moon. TRUE/FALSE

If it's completely dark...
3 Your face wouldn't appear in a mirror. TRUE/FALSE

4 You couldn't take holiday snaps. TRUE/FALSE
5 A poisonous rattlesnake couldn't find where you are hiding. TRUE/FALSE

1 TRUE. A rainbow happens when sunlight shines through droplets of rain. This splits the sunlight into different colours. (Check out pages 28-32 for the colourful details.) You actually get rainbows at night made by moonlight but the colours are too dim for your eyes to make out.

2 TRUE. The moon doesn't make its own light. That pretty silvery moonlight is actually sunlight that's bounced off (or as a scientist might say, reflected from) the moon. The surface of the moon is made of rock and dust but if it was ice it would reflect light really well and the moon would be nearly as bright as the sun.

3 TRUE. A mirror works by reflecting light. There's nothing to stop you looking at the bathroom mirror in the dark. But since there's no light the mirror won't reflect your image. Mind you, according to legend, if you're a vampire the mirror won't show your image anyway.

4 TRUE. Imagine you went pot-holing in a dark cave and left your torch at home. Whoops. You couldn't take any snaps because the chemicals that make a photograph only work if light falls on the film.

5 FALSE. The rattlesnake has a pit on each side of its head full of temperature sensors. These detect heat from your body. It's frightening. And that's why hiding from the snake in a dark cupboard isn't such a clever idea.

THE LIGHT FANTASTIC

So light brightens up your life, but take a closer look at light and it becomes even more fantastic... Imagine you could look at a ray of light through an incredibly powerful microscope. It would have to be billions of times more powerful than the world's most powerful microscope. Here's what you might see.

Photons are never still – they whiz along in the form of light waves. And hundreds of light waves could stretch across this full stop.

Photons sound phenomenal, don't they? You can imagine them as tiny little super-heroes flying through the air

14

with awesome powers – so here's a story about one of them. Ooops – before you read it, I ought to tell you that an atom is a tiny ball of matter. Everything in the known universe – including you and me and this book – are made of different combinations of different types of atom.

Continued overleaf...

But the most incredible thing about Super-Photon isn't his super-hero powers – it's the fact that he's *nothing special*. You make photons all the times by zapping atoms with energy – for example by heating. That's why the toaster element glowed red when you burnt the toast this morning and that's why bulbs glow when you switch on the light. What happens is the cloud of electrons that whiz around the centre of an atom spit out photons in the form of light waves.

Each light wave is actually made up of a linked electric and a magnetic wave moving in the same direction. And since you can't get one without the other scientists lump them together and say that a light wave is a form of electromagnetic wave.

Bet you never knew!

1 The more energy you blast an atom with the more times the light wave will wiggle per second. And if you want to sound like a scientist you say "I am increasing the frequency of the electromagnetic waves".

2 At lower levels of energy you make radio waves, but turn up the power and you'll make different colours of light (from red going up to violet). Turn it up a bit more and you make ultraviolet light – a kind of high-energy light that you can't see. Keep going to maximum levels and you blast out deadly gamma rays.

3 You might wonder what happens to photons after they hit something. Well, remember a photon is just a blip of energy. It hits an atom and its energy is soaked up. So it's bye-bye photon. But photons do much more than whiz around...

Dare you discover ... what light can do?

To begin with:

Wrap some kitchen foil round the end of a small bright torch.

MAKE SURE THE BATTERIES ARE WORKING!

TORCH

KITCHEN FOIL (SHINY SIDE FACING THE TORCH)

ELASTIC BAND TO HOLD FOIL IN PLACE

2MM WIDE HOLE MADE BY A PENCIL POINT

You will need:

YOUR TORCH PREPARED AS SHOWN

ERK! IT'S MILKY AND MURKY!

A SQUARE BOTTLE OR STORAGE JAR WITH 9CM OF WATER. ADD A DROP OF MILK IN WITH THE WATER AND STIR. THE WATER SHOULD BE VERY SLIGHTLY CLOUDY, BUT STILL SEE-THROUGH.

9CM

Experiment 1:
1 Place the jar in front of a dark object. A dark book or some gloomy wallpaper will do.
2 Put your torch up the sides of the jar and switch on the light. You should be able to see the beam of light.
3 Now shine the light up so it hits the underside of the water.

What do you notice?
a) The light seems to flicker like a dodgy TV.
b) The light dances sideways.
c) The light seems to bounce down at an angle.

Experiment 2:
Now place the torch about 5 cm away from the sides of the jar. Try shining the light up or down from different angles.

What do you notice?
a) From some angles the light beam suddenly jumps to one side as it passes through the sides of the jar.
b) The water begins to heat up and bubble as you move the light.
c) No matter how you move the torch the light beam is always a straight line.

Answers:
1 c) The light bounces (reflects) off the underside of the water. The surface of the water is very smooth and the photons of light can all reflect in the same direction.
2 a) Light doesn't always go in a straight line. When light travels from air to water it slows to 224,900 km per second. This is because the photons have to push through lots of atoms in the water – just imagine a crowd of people trying to run.

through another crowd. When a beam of light hits the water at an angle one side of the beam slows before the other. This makes the beam bend

FRIGHTENING EXPRESSIONS

One astronomer says to another...

Is this ref action something to do with a football match?

Answer:
No. Scientists call the bending of light refraction (re-frak-tion).

By now you'll have realized...

1 There's more to light than meets the eye.
2 That light is horribly amazing.

But you might also feel puzzled. If photons are so tiny and so fast how come scientists know so much about them? I mean, you can't exactly catch photons in a butterfly net. Well, it took the combined brain power of some frighteningly bright scientists to discover the truth.

TURN THE PAGE AND DISCOVER HOW THEY DID IT...

HORRIBLY BRIGHT SCIENTISTS

Much of our knowledge of light is based on the work of two scientific geniuses, Isaac Newton (1642–1727) and Albert Einstein (1879–1955). However, lots of scientists lent a hand. Well, as they say "many hands make LIGHT work", ha ha. Here's a handy spotter's guide to scientists who study light.

Spot the scientist

1. Physicists (Fizzy-cists)

INTERESTED IN: physical forces that shape the world – stuff like heat or electricity. The actual type of physicist featured in this book is an optical physicist. And – you guessed it – they study light.

WHAT THEY DO: set up experiments, make calculations about the speed of light and other exciting topics.

WHERE THEY WORK: university laboratories.

SPOTTER'S NOTE: physicists can be rather scruffy and absent-minded about their clothes. This is because they're too busy thinking about complex experiments to worry about how they look.

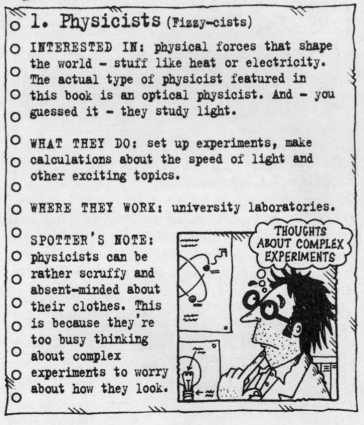

THOUGHTS ABOUT COMPLEX EXPERIMENTS

2. Astronomers

INTERESTED IN: stars and planets and other things you find in outer space. Astronomers are interested in light because we can only see space objects because of the light they produce or reflect.

WHAT THEY DO: scan the night sky using telescopes.

WHERE THEY WORK: observatories.

SPOTTER'S NOTE: astronomers are shy creatures that hide away in remote mountain-top observatories – but you can spot them in science conferences

CLOSE-UP OF RARE PHOTO SHOWING ASTRONOMER CREEPING OUT TO HER OBSERVATORY AT NIGHT

3. Ophthalmologists (op-thal-mol-ogists)

INTERESTED IN: eyeballs, their diseases and how they work.

WHAT THEY DO: they're trained doctors who treat patients with eye problems. Some are surgeons who perform operations on the eye.

WHERE THEY WORK: hospital eye departments.

SPOTTER'S NOTE: it's hard to find an ophthalmologist because they're always busy. Loads of people have sight problems, you see?

HAVE YOU SEEN HIM YET?

IF I COULD SEE HIM I WOULDN'T BE HERE

OPHTH

PULLING A FAST ONE

For centuries scientists were keen to measure the speed of light. They knew that this would help them judge the distance of planets and so make more accurate astronomical observations. So loads of scientists had a go. But they had a problem. Light is kind of speedy. All light photons belt along at 299,792,458 metres a second. There's nothing faster in the known universe – not even kids leaving a science class on a Friday afternoon.

Now, you'd think it would be impossible to clock the speed of light. I mean, you'd need amazingly quick reactions and a very good stopwatch to do it – right? So how did scientists manage this impossible feat? First off the mark was Italian scientist Galileo Galilei (1564–1642).

GALLANT GALILEO

One dark night Galileo and a friend went into the mountains. Each man carried a lantern with a shutter.

Galileo climbed a hill. His friend climbed another hill three kilometres away. It was a cold, lonely and dangerous trek and if either man had fallen there was no hope of a quick rescue.

Once he reached the top of his hill Galileo opened the shutter of his lantern and started counting. The plan was for the friend to show his lantern in response to Galileo's signal.

To his relief Galileo saw the light from his friend's lantern and stopped counting.

COULD YOU BE A SCIENTIST?

But great Galileo was wrong – as he found out when he and his long-suffering pal tried climbing hills further apart. Light is so speedy that a few squitty kilometres make no obvious difference to the measurements. Galileo was simply timing how quickly he reacted to the light signals. He realised this and gave up.

LIGHT SPEED CLOCKED

Using complex calculations, astronomers were also trying to clock the speed of light. In 1676 Danish stargazer Ole Roemer (1644–1710) was watching Jupiter's moon Io when he figured out that the further away Earth was from Jupiter, the longer it took light to reach his telescope. Using Roemer's data, scientists reckoned that light travelled at about 225,000 km per second. Not bad – but not right. Then in 1725 British astronomer James Bradley came up with a new figure using brain-blistering sums such as the angle of his telescope and the speed of the Earth. He was just five per cent out.

Meanwhile, back in the hills. In 1849 French physicist Armand Fizeau (1819–1896) shone a bright light from the top of a hill. The light shone through the spokes of a spinning wheel and bounced off a mirror on a hilltop eight km distant before returning through the wheel.

I WORKED OUT THE SPEED OF LIGHT BY MEASURING THE DISTANCE THE WHEEL TRAVELLED, ITS SPEED AND THE DISTANCE LIGHT TRAVELLED

THAT'S 'WHEELY' CLEVER!

His figure of 313,300 km per second was a bit too speedy. But the technique proved to be a bright idea and was used by other scientists.

Bet you never knew!

In 1926 and 1929 American Albert Michelson (1852–1931) performed similar tests using a rapidly turning mirror instead of a wheel.

MIRRORS

MIRROR FACE

LIGHT SOURCE

THE TURNING MIRROR TURNS ROUND BY ONE FACE AND THE LIGHT BOUNCES OFF THE ROUND MIRROR 35 KM (21 MILES) AWAY

Michelson's measurements of the distance the light travelled and the speed of his mirror were more accurate than Fizeau's. But Albert's final result was still wrong – too slow by just 18 km a second. Ooops. Modern estimates use a similar approach but more accurate clocks and lasers mean the whole experiment can be controlled more precisely. So you get a more accurate measurement.

IZZY THE INCREDIBLE

One scientist played a key role in bringing the secrets of light to light – he was Isaac Newton. Of course, any old teacher will tell you that Newton is famous for describing the fatal forces that can affect a moving object – forces such as gravity. But do they also know that Newton's pet dog was named Diamond? Now Diamond wasn't quite as smart as his brainy owner. Here's what his diary might have looked like if he'd learnt to write.

A dog's diary

by Diamond

Cambridge ~ 2 June 1664

My master, Isaac is grumpy today. Oh well, so what — he's a miserable human. Mind you his bark is worse than his bite — ha ha. Actually, Isaac's mum is to blame. Isaac and I are at College but Isaac's skint. Isaac's mum is really rich but she never sends us any pocket money. So poor Isaac has to earn a few pennies by working as a waiter in the College. Then he's allowed to eat the scraps and leftovers. And guess what I get? Isaac's scraps and leftovers.

YUK!

Oh well, it's a dog's life.

31 August

Isaac is barking mad. (Well mad, anyway.) We went to a fair but instead of buying a nice juicy joint of meat for me, Isaac spent his hard-earned pennies on a prism. Well, he calls it a "prism". I call it a stupid triangular lump of glass that you can't even eat. So I whimpered in protest.

Isaac looked down at me in surprise.

"Are you OK?" he asked.

My master often talks to me because he doesn't have too many human friends.

"I'm rough," I replied.

Actually it sounded more like "ruff!" so Isaac ignored me. Well, he's still working and I'm dog-tired. So I'm taking my grumbling belly off to bed.

Woolsthorpe, Lincolnshire ~ 25 December 1665

We're here staying with Isaac's mum. It's all to do with something called "the plague". Well, humans are dropping dead like flies and the College is closed. So we came here. It's a good thing this plague. Now I get fed regularly by Isaac's mum. Yum, yum – Christmas goose bones.

1 January 1666

My master missed supper ... again. As usual, he's up in his room scribbling masses of meaningless numbers and mumbling scientific gibberish about light. He never washes or changes his clothes – phwoar, he's really going to the dogs. Mind you, I'm always ready to help my master. That's why I made sure I was at hand to eat his supper for him. At least it didn't go to waste!

12 January

I sneaked into Isaac's room today. Got a bit of a shock. Isaac has made a small hole in the shutters. (I bet his mum will have a fit when she sees the damage.) A ray of light shone through the hole and made a blob of sunlight on the wall. This proves my theory — Isaac *is* completely bonkers.

13 January

Lovely crisp, sunny morning — perfect for walkies. So I bounded into Isaac's room joyfully barking and wagging my tail. And guess what I saw? A bright beam of sunlight shone through that funny hole and on to that useless glass prism. The light shone out of the prism and hit the wall and the wall was covered in colours. Weird. It looked like a rainbow.

Well, at first I thought "Cor — that's a neat bit of painting," but then I realized the colours

funny hole

prism

white light

rainbow

were made by the light. "Maybe that prism has magical powers," I thought.

Then I saw the broad grin on Isaac's face.

"What do you think of the rainbow, Diamond?" he whispered excitedly, pressing his face up close.

"Woof!" I replied. This is usually the best response when Isaac gets worked up about something.

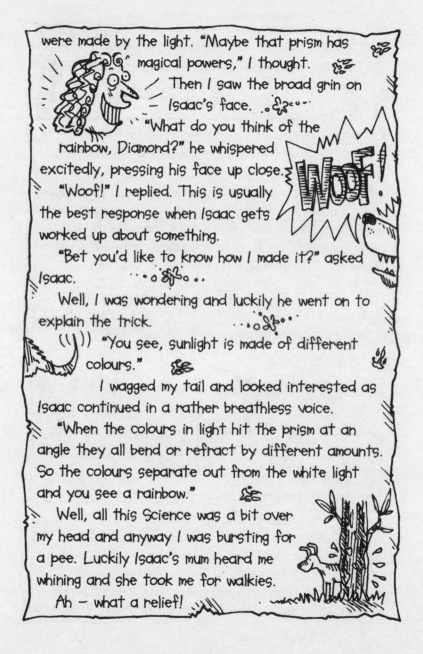

"Bet you'd like to know how I made it?" asked Isaac.

Well, I was wondering and luckily he went on to explain the trick.

"You see, sunlight is made of different colours."

I wagged my tail and looked interested as Isaac continued in a rather breathless voice.

"When the colours in light hit the prism at an angle they all bend or refract by different amounts. So the colours separate out from the white light and you see a rainbow."

Well, all this Science was a bit over my head and anyway I was bursting for a pee. Luckily Isaac's mum heard me whining and she took me for walkies.

Ah – what a relief!

BLAZING A TRAIL

Although Isaac wasn't the first person to make a rainbow using a prism he was the first to prove colours are part of sunlight and not somehow made by the glass. He did this by shining red light from his "rainbow" through a second prism and finding that it didn't split any further.

Isaac had blazed a trail in Science but his work sparked a blazing row. He sent an account of it to the Royal Society (that's the club for top scientists founded in 1662) but rival scientist Robert Hooke (1635–1703) claimed that Isaac's experiments didn't work properly. In fact, the glass in Hooke's prism probably wasn't as clear as Newton's so he couldn't get the same results. But as a result of the row Newton stopped speaking to Hooke.

Isaac also suffered in another kind of blaze. He returned to Cambridge after the plague but one Sunday he went to church leaving a candle burning in his laboratory. Perhaps Diamond wanted to try a few experiments too. Anyway, he jumped on the table, knocked over the candle and started a fire. According to one report, the blaze destroyed all Isaac's notes on light and all his chemistry equipment. I expect poor Diamond ended up in the dog house.

Isaac rewrote his notes from memory. But he didn't publish any of his work until 1704. By this time Hooke was dead so Isaac got the last word on light. Except, of course, it wasn't the last word. Isaac had reckoned light was made of tiny balls. But there was no way he could see the balls so his idea is a bit of a stab in the dark – ha ha. And within a century a brilliant scientist would see the problem in a different light.

Hall of fame: Thomas Young (1773–1829) Nationality: British

Young Tom Young was frighteningly clever. He was so brilliant at school that the whole class probably wanted to sit next to him in Science tests. He learnt to read when he was two. By the time he was six he'd read the Bible – twice. By the time he was 14 he was designing telescopes and microscopes with the help of a friendly teacher. By then he could speak four languages besides English and he decided (no doubt as a bit of light relief) to teach himself eight more.

I'LL LEARN RUSSIAN, POLISH AND CHINESE. . . THEN I'LL HAVE LUNCH

Tom trained as a doctor but in 1797 his uncle died and left him a fortune. This was good news. Well, not for the uncle, but good news for Tom. At last he could afford to do what he really wanted – lots of lovely science experiments.

Unfortunately few people got to hear of Tom's discoveries. His articles were so boring that not many people bothered to read them. Not surprising really – Tom was sacked from a job at the Royal Institution because his lectures were too dull. (Note: this is unlikely to happen to your teacher. So stop daydreaming and get on with this book.)

YOU'RE SACKED FOR DULL TEACHING, MR BROWN! TELL YOUR CLASS TO TAKE THE REST OF THE DAY OFF.

DRONE, WITTER, DRONE

In 1803 Tom proved that light takes the form of light waves. This was quite an achievement because as you know light waves are too small to see – 14,000 light waves could stretch across your thumbnail. In fact, the idea of light waves wasn't totally new. It had been put forward in 1690 by Dutch astronomer Christiaan Huygens (1629-1695) who based his suggestion on complex maths. But it was Thomas Young who dreamt up the experiment that proved light waves really exist.

Here's how he did it...

1. Firstly, I shone a light through a slit in a screen

SLIT   LIGHT   SCREEN

2. The light passed through two slits side by side in a second screen and spread out.

SECOND SCREEN WITH TWO SLITS

3. I knew I was on the right lines when the two beams of light merged to form a pretty pattern of bright and dark lines and colours.

PROJECTED ONTO SCREEN

4 Tom was able to show how this pattern was made by waves of light spreading out from the two slits. The two sets of waves spread out and passed through each other. Where the waves got in each other's way they made shadows – those were the dark lines.

Remember that light contains different colours? Where two light waves only partly blocked each other's way you saw the colours made by the waves that got through. But at the points the two sets of light waves actually managed to pass through one another you saw them both. This made the bright lines. Got all that?

FRIGHTENING EXPRESSIONS

One physicist says to another...

HOW'S YOUR DIFFRACTION?

I'M WORRIED ABOUT INTERFERENCE.

So who's interfering with the action?

> **Answer:**
> Hopefully, no one. **1.** Diffraction means light waves spreading out after passing through a narrow gap. **2.** Interference is a posh word for the effect that Young saw when two waves meet and either make a brighter light or colours or block one another out. (This effect turns up in the oddest places – keep an eye open for it in the rest of this book.)

THE FINAL, FINAL WORD?

More evidence built up to show that light took the form of waves and that Huygens and Young were right. For example, in 1818 French physicist Augustin Jean Fresnel (1788-1827) used brilliant maths to show how light waves can produce reflections and refraction. But was light really nothing more than a collection of waves? Was Newton's idea of light just a load of nonsense?

In 1901 German physicist Max Planck (1858-1947), spoilt the party. Planck said light is actually made of blips of energy called "quanta" (kwan-ta). Max's figures explained how the energy of light can be turned into heat inside a black box. But the only way his calculations added up was if light comes in quanta. These quanta are now called photons.

Four years later a scientific mega-genius used maths to prove Planck right. He performed no experiments and used only a pen and notepad for calculations. But he was able to prove that light was made up of photons, but that each blip moves so fast it forms a light wave. This idea was gradually accepted by physicists.

So who was this extraordinary scientist?

EXTRAORDINARY EINSTEIN

Albert Einstein is best known for his theories of relativity which he came up with in 1905 and 1915.

I HAVE PROVED THAT TIME AND SPACE ARE THE SAME THING AND THAT TIME CAN BE AFFECTED BY SPEED

If you haven't a clue what he's talking about, don't worry – you're not alone. There's a good chance that your teacher isn't aware of the finer details either.

BUT WHAT DOES HE MEAN, MISS?

ER, THAT'S ENOUGH SCIENCE FOR TODAY, ...GET YOUR READING BOOKS OUT

Of course, most well-informed teachers can tell you that Einstein was born in Germany, that he made his 1905 discoveries whilst working in Switzerland, and that from the 1930s he lived in America. But here's five facts they probably don't know about awesome Albert.

1 Einstein got interested in light at the age of 14 when he was daydreaming (no doubt during a particularly boring Science lesson). He imagined he was riding on top of a beam of light.

BEAM ME UP, SCOTTY!

This was dangerous (that's daydreaming, not riding on light – as you know, it's impossible to surf on light). In those days, the punishment for not paying attention was a whack across the knuckles with a cane. History doesn't record whether Albert suffered this punishment but he probably did.

2 Einstein was eventually expelled from school. His teacher couldn't stand the sight of him lolling at the back of the class and smiling and not doing any work. But Einstein was a genius and he was more interested in his own studies. (The chances are you won't get away with this excuse.)

IT'LL TAKE MORE THAN NOT COMBING YOUR HAIR TO MAKE YOU A GENIUS, JENKINS

3 Some people think that Einstein's discoveries about light were actually made by Mileva Einstein – Albert's first wife. Albert once remarked:

EVERYTHING I HAVE CREATED AND ATTAINED I OWE TO MILEVA

However their son, Hans Albert, explained that although Mileva helped with the maths it was Albert who did the scientific thinking. Albert probably meant that having Mileva to look after him gave him the time and confidence to develop his ideas.

4 After Einstein's death, a doctor removed the great man's brain, sliced it into little bits and stored it in a couple of large jars. His aim was to give it away to researchers into genius. At one point the doctor and reporter drove across the USA to present the sliced-up brain to Einstein's grand-daughter. But she didn't want the grily relic.

ALBERT EINSTEIN (GENIUS)

ALBERT SHUTTLEWORTH (DIMWIT)

5 At the same time as his brain was taken, the doctor removed his eyeballs as souvenirs.

Would you want souvenirs like these? Probably not, and if squelching bloodshot eyeballs make you shudder you might want to close your own eyes before you turn the page.

Because the next chapter is *bulging* with them...

BULGING EYEBALLS

Here's a really FRIGHTENING thought. Imagine one morning you opened your eyes and saw nothing – just darkness. As black as the darkest night without even a glimmer of starlight. You'd be in a blind panic, wouldn't you? (Or you might think it actually was night and go back to sleep.)

Well, thank goodness for eyeballs. If it wasn't for them you wouldn't be able to see any light at all.

BULGING EYEBALLS QUIZ

If you're itching to know more about eyeballs, there's one opposite that's been freshly cut in half. In this quiz each part of the eyeball has a matching fact. All you have to do is match the bits of eyeball to the relevant facts...

EYEBALL BITS AND PIECES

1 Ciliary muscles
2 Iris
3 Optic nerve
4 Retina with rod and cone cells*

5 Cornea
6 Eyelashes
7 Lens
8 Watery bit
9 Sclera (sk-leer-a)
10 Eye muscles

*By the way the "cells" are more than 50 trillion tiny living jelly-like blobs that make up your body. But you probably knew that already.

RELEVANT FACTS

a) There are 200 of these.

b) This bit helps to keep the eyeball in shape.

c) They stop your eyeball slopping out of its socket.

d) The colour of this bit stops light getting through and dazzling you.

e) This bit is 6.5 square cm (one square inch). Without it you'd see nothing.

f) This bit changes shape 100,000 times a day.

g) This bit controls the eyeball part mentioned in **f)**.

h) This part sucks in oxygen gas from the air.

i) There are one million fibres in this bit.

j) You can see the blood vessels in this bit.

Answers:

1g) 2d) Light goes through the pupil – the hole in the middle. (The colour of your eye doesn't make any difference to what you see.) **3i)** They're nerve fibres. Their job is to take the pattern of light signals picked up by the retina to the brain in the form of nerve signals. **4e)** It's got 4.5 million cone cells to give you colour vision and about 90 million rod cells that detect light but not colours. (For more info. on colour vision see page 134.) **5h)** The cornea has no blood vessels to supply it with the sugar and oxygen it needs to stay alive. It gets sugars from the gloopy fluid in the eye and oxygen directly from the air. **6a)** They fall out after about three months, but you always grow more.

ERK! MY EYELIDS ARE GOING BALD!

7f) The lens thickens or lengthens so that light from whatever you are looking at is bent (refracted) and so focused on the retina. That's blinking amazing, isn't it? **8b)** Yes, it's true, you're looking at this page through a pool of watery jelly. **9j)** It's the "white" of your eyeball. When the eyeball is injured or has a disease the blood vessels get inflamed and get bigger. And the eyeball looks gungey and bloodshot. **10c)** They also swivel the eyeball round to look at things. Your brain coordinates the muscles on each eyeball so they work together. When this doesn't happen you go cross-eyed.

Bet you never knew!
1 The way your retina lets you see light is horribly complicated. When you look at something, photons of light hit the cells in the retina. These cells contain coloured chemicals called pigments. The photons spark a series of chemical reactions first in the pigments and then in the cells. These create a nerve signal that travels to the brain. And get this – all this confusing chaotic chemistry happens more or less instantly. And all the time.
2 So how good are your eyeballs? Are they sharp as needles or a sight for sore eyes? Why not put them through their paces? Your eyeballs should be good enough to spot a coin in the playground at 65 metres. Better make sure the playground is empty before trying this experiment, though.

Now for another eyeball test.

Dare you discover ... how something horrible appears to happen to your hand?

You will need:

One red piece of A4 paper

One left hand (Go on use your own, it won't hurt ... honest!)

What you do:

1 Roll the paper lengthways into a tube 2.5 cm across.

2 Stand with a window on your right.

3 Put the tube to your right eye. Stare hard with both eyes open.

4 Place your left hand against the left side of the tube with your thumb underneath the tube.

What do you notice?

a) Your hand ... has disappeared.

b) Agggh! A bleeding hole has appeared in your hand.

c) Oh no! You've got two left hands.

Answer:

b) Your left and your right eyes are seeing different views. Your brain combines them to make a 3-D scene. This is what happens all the time when you look at things but in this case the scene is a rather horrible illusion.

But talking about dark conditions...

TEACHER'S TEA-BREAK TEASER

This teaser works best in a dark, sinister, gloomy corridor (most schools have a few). You'll need a book with very small print. (Try using a boring science book, not this one, obviously.) Knock on the staffroom door. When the door opens smile sweetly and ask...

Enjoy watching your teacher struggling with the tiny print. Then ask them why people can't read in the dark.

Answer:

This is a particularly fiendish teaser because there are actually two possible answers.

1 Your cone cells can detect light photons but there are not enough to form an image of the text.

2 Your poor old retina does its best. It tries to detect as many light photons as it can – but to do this it has to make use of rod cells covering a wider area than it would normally use to read. And because the retina is responding to light from this wider area it's hard for you to concentrate on tiny words.

Does your teacher know both answers?

COULD YOU BE A SCIENTIST?

Of course, these vital facts about vision didn't discover themselves. Scientists and doctors had to find them out by careful investigation. The discovery of how the lens in your eye focuses light was made by Thomas Young in 1792 using a real eyeball.

But where did it come from?

a) AN OX

b) A GOLDFISH

c) AN EXECUTED CRIMINAL

48

Answer:
a) He cut the eyeball in half and shone a light through the pupil. He could then see how the lens helped to focus light.

TEST YOUR TEACHER

You can liven up a boring swimming lesson by asking this tricky science question. It's sure to make a big splash.

*WHY DOES EVERYTHING APPEAR
BLURRED UNDER WATER?

Answer:
Normally light refracts (that's bends, remember) as it passes through the cornea. This bending happens as light passes from the air into the watery cornea. This helps to bend light on to the retina allowing you to see things in focus.

49

When you're underwater the light is already going through water so it doesn't bend into the cornea. As a result the light isn't so well focused on your retina and things appear blurred.

FRIGHTENING EXPRESSIONS
An ophthalmologist asks...

Answer:
No. Accommodation is the way your ciliary muscles change the lens shape to focus light. The lens gets shorter and fatter when you look at things that are near, and longer and thinner for objects that are further away. Like the cornea this makes the light from these objects refract and focus on your retina. Accommodation problems might cause you to bump into teachers or lampposts (see page 116 for more details).

Talking about eye problems, take a very close look at this (if you can).

Dear Doc...

Each week Dr Scalpel answers your health questions. This week. . .

PROBLEMS WITH THE EYEBALLS

Dear Doc,
I'm a football linesman with TERRIBLE eyesight. I can't always spot when a player is offside. I should explain, Doc, that "offside" means collecting

Continued →

a forward pass with no opponents
between you and the goal line when
the ball is kicked. And it's not
allowed. But as I said, I'm not
always sure when a player is
offside. You see, they move so
fast it's very confusing. And when I
make the wrong decision the fans
call me rude names. It's so hurtful
... I could cry.
Should I retire?

Mr I.B. Worried

Dear Mr Worried
Cheer up – your eyesight is normal. In 1998
eye specialists in Madrid, Spain found that
it takes 300 milliseconds for an eye to
focus on a moving footballer. Meanwhile
the player might have moved two or more
metres. So it's hard to be sure when a
footballer's offside. Well, Mr Worried, this
embarrassing secret is safe with me and the
200,000 readers of the *Daily Searchlight*.

PS Funny how fans can always spot when a
player from the opposing team is offside.

Dear Doc

I keep seeing dark dots in front of my eyes – am I going dotty?

I.C. Spottes

Dear Mr Spottes

The dots you describe are probably caused by blood clots on your retina. A larger dark spot may be caused by damage to your retina. In both cases you should see a doctor. I'm sure they'll spot the problem.

Dear Doc

My eyesight is gradually disappearing round the edges of my field of vision. When I look at a light I see a blurred halo around it. "Halo, halo, halo," I said to myself – I must be seeing things. What do you think?

Mrs N.D. Dark

Dear Mrs Dark

You sound like you might have glaucoma (gly-comb-a). The watery gloop in your eyeball is produced behind your iris. For reasons we doctors don't understand, you can make too much gloop. It builds up inside your eyeball pressing outwards until it squeezes your optic nerve – that's the nerve that takes signals from your retina to your brain. This reduces vision and causes blindness. But don't panic! You can take drops to cut the amount of gloop your eye makes and relieve the pressure on your nerve.

That's a relief – eh?

Dear Doc
Please help me - I think I'm going blind. My eyesight is blurred and dim. I keep seeing double. What's happening to me?

Ms Rabble

Dear Ms Rabble

You could have a cataract. A build up of fluid in the lens leads to chemical changes that cause a cloudy area. Seeing double happens when two cloudy areas refract light from the same object. Fortunately the cataract can be removed in a simple operation.

PS One traditional remedy for cataracts was to plop a warm drop of pee (or urine, as we doctors call it) into the eye. Don't try this – it's useless and may cause infection.

> **DON'T MISS NEXT WEEK.** It 'snot' much fun having problems with your nostrils. **Dear Doc** looks into noses...

There's lots of possible causes for cataracts, including damage to the lens after being outside too much under the huge sizzling blinding solar nuclear explosion in the sky.

The what?

The sun, of course.

It's time to put on those shades and turn the page...

SIZZLING SUNSHINE

We're all lucky people. Every day we get hours and hours of free sunshine. Well, OK, that's true for California and it's not quite so true if you're snowed up in Siberia. But even when the weather's grotty – cheer up – the sun's shining up there above the clouds providing warmth and light. And all for free!

But the sun is more than a big light bulb in the sky. The whole future of life on Earth depends on the sun. This fact is so basic even aliens know about it...

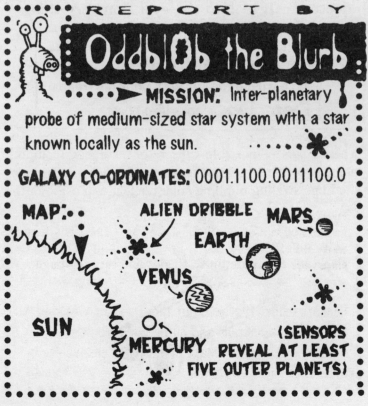

REPORT BY

Oddbl☼b the Blurb

▶ **MISSION:** Inter-planetary probe of medium-sized star system with a star known locally as the sun.

GALAXY CO-ORDINATES: 0001.1100.0011100.0

MAP:

ALIEN DRIBBLE   MARS

EARTH

VENUS

SUN

MERCURY   (SENSORS REVEAL AT LEAST FIVE OUTER PLANETS)

INTELLIGENT LIFE ◄

A species known as humanoids are very abundant on Planet Earth. We have captured a specially trained humanoid known as a "Science teacher" for further research. The names given to planets in this report are names used by the humanoid.

Science teacher – emitted squeaky sound like, "ARR-YOR-AN-ALEEE-EN!"

STAR STATUS ◄

The sun is in the middle of its life. It is 4.5 billion years old. The centre is 14,000,000° C (27,000,000° F). Light photons are produced by atoms as they are fused together. Just like any other star of this type, really.

PLANET EARTH ◄

This planet is the only one suitable for life. Life on planet Earth depends on light from the sun.

PLANTS – GREEN NON-MOVING LIFE FORMS. PLANTS USE ENERGY FROM SUNLIGHT TO TURN WATER AND CARBON DIOXIDE GAS FROM AIR INTO FOOD.

SUN
– ENERGY

HUMANOIDS EAT ANIMALS AND PLANTS.

ANIMALS – MOBILE LIFE FORMS THAT EAT PLANTS OR OTHER ANIMALS.

Sensors report that without the sun there would be no plants, no animals and humanoids would be missing out on their intake of nutritive chemicals otherwise known as lunch.

INVASION POTENTIAL ◀ • • • • • • • • • •

Planet Earth is suitable for invasion – but from our study of the Science teacher we have established that humans spend much of their time communicating boring information. Life on Earth may prove unbearably dull for higher forms of intelligence such as Blurbs. So we have erased the humanoid's memory of our visit and put him back where we found him.

ZONK!...now where was I...ah yes, your science homework, Smith...

AWESOME ECLIPSES

One dramatic effect of the sun is called an eclipse. This is caused by the moon getting in the way of the sun's light so that its shadow falls on the Earth.

Oh, so you knew that? Well, in the past many people didn't – so they made up stories and performed rituals to make sense of what was going on.

1 An eclipse can be frightening. If you don't know what's happening, it looks like the moon is swallowing the sun. According to ancient Greek writer Thucydides (460-400 BC) an eclipse halted a battle in Persia in the sixth century BC. The two armies drew back and agreed to go on with the battle after a month, when any bad magical effects had worn off.

2 In ancient China people thought a dragon was eating the sun and banged gongs or pans to scare the monster away.

59

3 The native peoples of North America fired flaming arrows at the sky in a bid to re-light the sun.

THIS IS AN 'ARROWING EXPERIENCE!

4 The Pampas tribes of South America believed the moon goddess was darkened in an eclipse with her own blood drawn by savage dogs. Of course, they were barking up the wrong tree.

5 Some Tartar tribes in Asia believed the sun and moon were swallowed up by a blood-sucking vampire from a distant star.

6 In many countries people thought (wrongly) that diseases spread during eclipses. The Yukon tribes of Alaska covered their pots and pans during eclipses for this reason. A terrible outbreak of 'flu that claimed thousands of victims in South America in 1918 was blamed by some on an eclipse.

Dare you discover ... how to observe an eclipse?

Eclipses of the sun are fairly rare. There are often less than five a year – so chances are, you won't be able to see one from your own backyard. To see one you might have to travel to far flung places like the North Pole. Well, when you get there, here's a way to watch the eclipse without hurting your eyes.

Note: If there aren't any eclipses coming up you can always use this method to look at the sun safely. You can try it at home in a shaft of bright sunlight.

You will need:
The sun (but of course!)
A large sheet of white paper and something to fix it to the wall with
A small mirror
Ruler
A piece of card
Scissors and sticky tape

What you do:
1 Cut a circle in the card 2.5 cm across.
2 Tape the card over the mirror and stick the paper on the wall in a dark shadowy corner.
3 Hold the mirror so that it reflects the sunlight from the circle onto the white paper. You'll see a nice image of the Sun that's safe to look at.

URGENT HORRIBLE HEALTH WARNING!

Staring at the sun is dangerous. Even a few moments of being blasted by the Sun's high-energy photons kills off cells in your retina and gazing at the Sun too long can cause cataracts and blindness. Any really bright light can be harmful Welders who don't use protective goggles get "arc eye" and go blind for a while – or even for ever. So you'd be blind stupid to risk it.

A SNAP DECISION
If you think the dangers of observing an eclipse sound

rather frightening, spare a thought for Warren de la Rue (1815-1889). In 1860 top astronomer Sir John Herschel (1792-1871) asked this intrepid British photographer to travel to Rivabellosa in Spain to photograph an eclipse and prove a scientific fact.

"So Warren got a nice sun tan and took a few holiday snaps. What's so risky about that?" I hear you ask.

Well, in 1860 cameras were in their infancy and travel was a bit more primitive. So this was quite an undertaking. Here's what Warren's letters home might have looked like...

17 July 1860
To Sir John Herschel
Kew Observatory, England

SPEW!

Dear Sir John,
Here I am at Rivabellosa and what a terrible journey it's been! I was seasick and throwing up during the voyage to Spain. And the hassle of getting the equipment to the village! As you know, the combined camera and telescope we're going to use is almost as tall as me and weighs a few tonnes. The village is hundreds of miles from the sea. And the roads here are tracks. I'm covered in dust and I had to spend a fortune hiring smelly bullock carts.

Is this really the best place to see the eclipse? Wasn't there anywhere else nearer?
Oh well, we're here now. I'll write soon.

Yours wearily,   ←Me

Warren

18 July 1860 at 2 am
To Sir John Herschel
Kew Observatory
England

Dear Sir John

I may not send this letter. But I can't sleep and I've got to sort out my thoughts. It's just that I'm really scared things won't work out tomorrow. I know you're keen to get pictures of the flares that you see during an eclipse. It would be great to get nice clear pictures and prove the flares come from the sun and not from the moon or the sky as some people think. But no one's ever got a decent photo of an eclipse. What happens if you can't see the flares? And if it's cloudy tomorrow I won't see anything anyway.

I can't stand it. . . I wish I'd never come to this miserable little village. I want to go home. I don't think I'll send this letter. It might scare you, Sir John, it certainly scares me.

Warren

PS It's all your fault I'm here at all.
PPS The locals are suspicious. Some of them think I've got magical powers. If only.

Meanwhile some of the people of Rivabellosa must have been wondering what was going on. Here's how events might have appeared to a young boy.

THE ECLIPSE BY PEDRO

Our teacher told us all about the eclipse. But the old people in our village said it would bring sickness and disaster. That's what Grandpa thought. He said the sweaty Englishman had a magic machine to make the sun go dark for as long as he wished.

The day of the eclipse was bright and sunny. I went up the hill with Grandpa to get a good view. Grandpa was still grumbling and saying no good will come of it. There were crowds of people. The Englishman had his machine set up — I could see the end of it sticking out the top of a shed like a giant gun.

Just before the eclipse, we saw the moon getting close to the sun. Then a horrible dark shadow appeared in the distance. It was the shadow of the moon. The darkness swept over the hills like a thunderstorm. Everything went grey. All the flowers closed up and birds started snoozing in the trees. It was just like evening so I started yawning.

"Bored already?" snapped Grandpa.

Then things got scary. Grandpa →

Little by little the sun was swallowed up by the moon until all you could see was a black glowing circle. Suddenly my hair stood on end — I was seriously worried. It was dark. The stars had come out.

64

Maybe Grandpa was right.

Perhaps the sun had gone for ever.

I grabbed hold of his hand.

Meanwhile the Englishman was acting crazy.

Shouting at his assistants and disappearing into the shed to work his giant machine. We heard him muttering things to himself.

"He's saying spells," whispered Grandpa.

So Grandpa got down on to his bony knees and started reciting prayers. But there was no sign of the sun.

Where was it?

The minutes dragged by...

Just then a bright bead of light appeared. It looked like a diamond ring around the dark moon. Everyone cheered. I found myself dancing up and down.

"It's a miracle!" cried Grandpa, struggling to his feet.

It began to get light. Soon the sun was shining again in the blue sky. The eclipse was scary but brilliant. No one got ill, nothing terrible happened. I wish we had an eclipse every week. It's much better than listening to Grandpa strumming his guitar and singing awful old songs.

18 July 1860 at 4 pm
To Sir John Herschel
Kew Observatory, England

Dear Sir John
It's over and I'm shattered. Completely drained. Well, I tried. I took 35 shots

65

including two when the sun was completely covered. But the pictures weren't as good as I'd expected. THEY WERE BETTER! LOADS BETTER! You can see everything. You can see the flares really clearly. It's blindingly obvious the flares are coming from the sun itself!!!

Thank you, Sir John, for sending me to this wonderful little village full of lovely people. Now for a giant party and everyone's invited!!

Love Warren xx
PS Wish you were here!

A scientist writes...

Spanish scientist Father Angelo Secchi (1818–1878) also took a series of photos of the eclipse. Father Secchi was over 400 km to the south-east but the flares in his pictures matched the ones taken by De La Rue. This was the final proof that the flares had definitely come from the sun.

DARK SECRETS

It gets dark during an eclipse because the moon casts its shadow over the Earth. You get a shadow any time a solid object blocks light. (That's how the climber on the Brocken Mountain made the "ghost".) Something that blocks light is described as opaque (o-payk). And you can use an opaque shape to make horrible shadows...

Dare you discover ... what lurks in the shadows?

You will need:
A pencil
A pair of scissors
A piece of black card. You can always paint a white piece of card black.
A piece of wire
Sticky tape
A small, bright torch
A room with light walls.

What you do:
1 Draw and cut out a monster shape.
2 Tape the wire to the bottom of the shape to make a handle.
3 Wait until it gets dark. Draw the curtains and switch on your torch. Place the torch about three metres from the wall.
4 Hold the wire so the shape is between the light and the wall. You can make brilliant sinister shadows. Hold on, sorry to spoil things, but this is a serious scientific experiment, after all. So...

What do you notice?

a) You moved the shape towards the wall and away from the torch. The shadow on the wall got larger.

b) When the shape is closer to the light it blocks more light. This throws a larger shadow on the wall.

c) As you moved the torch the shadow began to move in the opposite direction. Help – it's alive!

Answer:

b) When the shape is closer to the light, it blocks more light. This throws a larger shadow on the wall. The larger shadow has more of a blurred edge than the smaller one. This is because some light from the edges of the torch can still shine past the edges of the shape, but not enough to give a sharp edge to the shadow.

HORRIBLE HEALTH WARNING!

This monster shape is ideal for scaring your little brother or sister. But you know it's wrong – don't you? And you're going to resist the temptation, aren't you? Well ... aren't you?

STRANGE STARLIGHT

Of course, astronomers aren't just interested in sunlight. They're also very excited by the topic of starlight. If you have secret ambitions to be an astronomer you might like to train your telescope on this next bit...

The stars are a long way off. A very long way off. You'll remember that sunlight takes about eight and a half minutes to reach us. But that's a blink of an eye for starlight. Even the light of our next door neighbour star Alpha Centauri takes four years to arrive. But that's nothing. If you live in the northern part of the world the most distant object you'll see is the Andromeda galaxy. The photons from this star cluster set off 2.2 million years before you were born. And you thought waiting for the school bus took for ever.

Astronomers are interested in starlight because without it they wouldn't be able to see stars. And by studying the colour of the light they can work out the surface temperature of the star. For example, a bluish white star is a sizzling 27,760°C and a red star is a nice cool 2,000°C. (OK, that's cool by star standards – the hottest temperatures on Earth include California's Death Valley which reached 49°C in 1917. Any hotter than that here and it would be Death Valley for the human race.)

The brightness of a star can also be used mathematically to work out its distance. This brilliant fact was noted by U.S. astronomer Henrietta Leavitt (1868–1921).

Bet you never knew!
Stars are coloured. It's true! The reason they seem white to us is that most stars are very dim. They only give your eye about 500 photons a second. This means that we can only see them with our dim light detecting rod cells. And the rod cells can't see colours, can they?

COULD YOU BE AN ASTRONOMER?

You've probably heard the rhyme:

Twinkle, twinkle little star
How I wonder what you are!

Next time you gaze at a star consider this puzzle:

Why do stars twinkle?

a) Because their light flashes on and off.

b) Because the starlight is refracted (bent) by gusts of wind.

c) Because fast-moving clouds keep blocking the light.

Answer:

b) As the wind blows, the atoms that make up air may get more crowded together in one area than another. As light passes through this area it refracts (bends) producing a twinkling effect. In fact, moonlight does this too but because the moon appears bigger to us you don't notice it twinkling around the edges.

Bet you never knew!

If you want to spot stars it helps if you live a long way away from the neighbours. In built-up areas the night sky often glows with the light of streetlights and shop signs reflecting off water droplets and dust in the air. This spoils the view of the twinkling stars.

But if lights are bad news for astronomers they're very good news for small frightened kids who are scared of the dark. So if you're reading this at dusk, maybe you'd better turn on the light before you switch to the next chapter.

It will brighten you ... and frighten you.

FRIGHTENING LIGHTING

This is a chapter about things that glow in the dark. And not all of them are light bulbs. Yep – long before anyone flicked a light switch, before even some bright spark invented fire, strange unearthly lights flickered in the darkness.

Intrigued? Let's bring the FRIGHTENING facts to light...

Frightening light fact file

NAME: Bioluminescence (bio-lum-min-nes-ance)

THE BASIC FACTS: 1. Certain living creatures can produce light.

2. Their bodies make a chemical called luciferin (loo-sif-fer-rin) and another called luciferase (loo-sif-fer-raze).

3. Luciferin combines with oxygen from the creature's blood and gives out light. Luciferase speeds up this chemical reaction.

THE FRIGHTENING DETAILS: Some bacteria do this. Some fish (see below) eat the bacteria. The bacteria remain alive and make light in the fish's skin.

'GLO' AWAY, YOU'RE UGLY!

THE GLOW IN THE DARK ZOO

Welcome to the world's first zoo where the animals provide the lighting...

Comb Jelly

Jelly-fish-like creature 25-30cm long.

FOUND IN: Pacific and Atlantic Oceans.

LIGHT IS USED FOR: scaring off attackers.

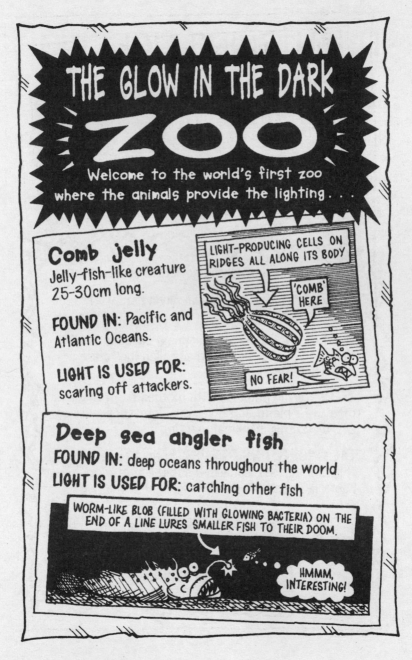

LIGHT-PRODUCING CELLS ON RIDGES ALL ALONG ITS BODY

'COMB' HERE

NO FEAR!

Deep sea angler fish

FOUND IN: deep oceans throughout the world

LIGHT IS USED FOR: catching other fish

WORM-LIKE BLOB (FILLED WITH GLOWING BACTERIA) ON THE END OF A LINE LURES SMALLER FISH TO THEIR DOOM.

HMMM, INTERESTING!

Fire flies and glow-worms

FOUND IN: fire flies live in North America and glow-worms live in Europe. Actually they're both varieties of beetle.

> PHWOAR! HE'S NICE!

FIRE FLY

LIGHT IS USED FOR: signalling for a mate.

> HERE I AM, BOYS!

Both insects have glowing lights on their bottoms. (Imagine you had one of these – you'd never need a rear bike light.)

GLOW-WORM

Luminous plankton

Tiny creatures often less than 1 mm long called copepods (cope-pods). The plankton also include plants called dinoflagellates (di-no- fladge-gell-ates).

COPEPOD

FOUND IN: every ocean especially where the water is rich in minerals.

LIGHT IS USED FOR: scaring away attackers. Ship toilets are often flushed with seawater – if the plankton are present they make your toilet glow in the dark. (Is this what they call a "flash in the pan"?)

> ARGH! WEIRD WEE WEE!

DINOFLAGELLATE

But there are other kinds of light around and these are not made by animals. Not living ones, anyway.

COULD YOU BE A SCIENTIST?

It's 200 years ago. You're walking home and you bravely decide to take a short cut through the graveyard. It's very dark – you're scared ... and suddenly you see an eerie glow. What's causing it?

a) It's a ghost. Yikes I'm out of here.

b) It's a mass of glow-worms feeding off rotting vegetation.

c) It's gases from a rotting body.

Answer:

c) Before new cemeteries were opened up in Victorian times many old churchyards became full up. Dead bodies were buried one on top of the other under a shallow layer of soil. Germs inside the rotting bodies made methane and phosphine (foz-feen) gas. As the gases reached the surface they often caught fire as a result of chemical reactions with oxygen in the air. The result was a pale blue glow that was called a will o' the wisp.

AWFUL ARTIFICIAL LIGHT

We take it for granted that by flicking a switch we can have light whenever we want. It's a part of every day life and without it you wouldn't be able to see this page, or even see to do homework (that would be tragic!). But just imagine you lived a few hundred years before there were light bulbs. Don't worry, you didn't have to use the glowing gas from a dead body. But the alternatives were almost as frightening.

Ye olde LIGHT UP YOUR LIFE home shopping catalogue

ROMANTIC CANDLES
Why not light your home with a genuine olde worlde candle as used by people since ancient Egyptian times. Wow, what a dazzling choice!

NOW WE HAVE TO WAIT 3500 YEARS FOR SOMEONE TO INVENT MATCHES

CONTINUED...

77

Traditional tallow candle

▷ Made with boiled up fat from around the kidneys of a dead cow, sheep or horse.

THE SMALL PRINT: Tallow candles are smelly and greasy. They go out easily and the pong is so bad that in parts of the West Indies the candles are lit to keep the bugs at bay.

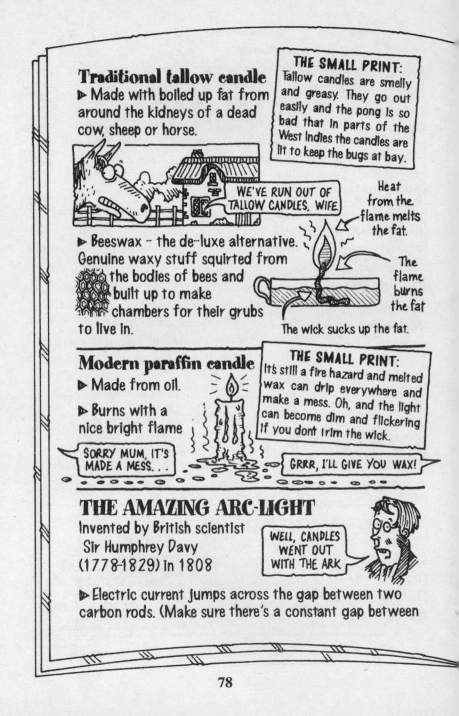

WE'VE RUN OUT OF TALLOW CANDLES, WIFE.

Heat from the flame melts the fat.

▷ Beeswax – the de-luxe alternative. Genuine waxy stuff squirted from the bodies of bees and built up to make chambers for their grubs to live in.

The flame burns the fat

The wick sucks up the fat.

Modern paraffin candle

▷ Made from oil.

▷ Burns with a nice bright flame

THE SMALL PRINT: It's still a fire hazard and melted wax can drip everywhere and make a mess. Oh, and the light can become dim and flickering if you dont trim the wick.

SORRY MUM, IT'S MADE A MESS...

GRRR, I'LL GIVE YOU WAX!

THE AMAZING ARC-LIGHT

Invented by British scientist Sir Humphrey Davy (1778-1829) in 1808

WELL, CANDLES WENT OUT WITH THE ARK

▷ Electric current jumps across the gap between two carbon rods. (Make sure there's a constant gap between

two carbon rods as the
light burns otherwise
the rods will melt or the
light will fizzle out.)

Electric current ↓ → Glowing carbon rod

THE SMALL PRINT: This light is a fire hazard. And it could blind you because it's brighter than 4,000 candles. The only practical use anyone ever found for it was in the Dungeness lighthouse. So unless your house happens to be a lighthouse it's probably not such a good idea.

TURN IT OFF!

GASLIGHT

As invented by Scottish inventor
William Murdock (1754-1839)

Flame made by burning coal gas

Handy tap to turn the gas on or off

ER - I'M JUST WARMING THE POT, MUM...

GRRR!

after an
experiment
in 1792
involving
heating coal
in his mum's
teapot.

THE SMALL PRINT:
You need pipes all over your house to carry the gas. And the gas is poisonous and can blow up your home. And even when it works the flame is smoky and smelly.

MARVELLOUS MODERN LIGHTS

Nowadays things are looking
much brighter. Go into any
street and you'll probably see
sodium or mercury street lights.
These work in roughly
the same way.

An electric current passes through the tube. Atoms in the gas take in energy and give out light.

Something else passing through a tube

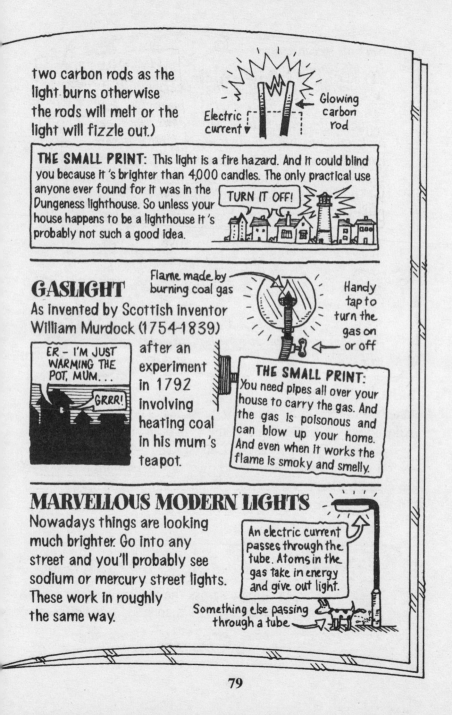

79

BRILLIANT BULBS

One invention put the others in the shade. The light bulb. And as every American knows the light bulb was invented by U.S. inventor Thomas A. Edison (1847–1931). And every well-informed Briton knows the light bulb was invented by British inventor Joseph Swan (1828–1914). So what's the truth?

Read on and find out...

Thomas A. Edison's diary

I've got this real smart idea for a new kind of light. All you do is send an electric current through a thin wire. This slows down the flow of electricity. The electric current drags along making the wire heat up and you get light. Simple but brilliant – like most of my inventions...

Hmm – need to pump out the air otherwise the thin wire will catch fire when you heat it up. You can't get fire without air – can you?

THIN WIRE

AIR IS MAKING THIN WIRE CATCH FIRE

ELECTRICITY

THE DAILY SUN

1 September 1878

Let there be light!

Brilliant inventor Thomas Edison is set to light up the world by inventing the light bulb. Already gas lighting company shares are plummeting at the prospect. And Edison hasn't even built a single bulb yet! But whiz-kid Edison is already famous for inventing the phonograph. (That's the new-fangled machine you can use to play music on.)

MR. T. EDISON

And now he's getting on with a bit of light work!

21 January 1879

If only I could make this light work. One day there could be a light bulb in every home. There might even be two in every home. I could become seriously rich. But only if everything goes to plan. I've hurt my eyes staring at the light bulbs... before they burnt out. Work is getting harder.

Those carbon filaments sure can burn. Seems my pumps aren't good enough to get all the air out of the bulbs. So I tried platinum wires instead - but they kept melting. Then I made a switch to cut the power if the platinum gets too hot but the light keeps flickering. Oh well - back to the drawing board. As I like to say, "inventing is 99 per cent perspiration and only 1 per cent inspiration".

1 April 1879

Did I say perspiration? Well, I'm in a cold sweat just now. To be precise, I'm at my wit's end. We've tried thousands of materials - rubber, fishing line, wood and now in desperation we're trying human hair. Two of my assistants volunteered to provide the hair. John Kruesli's got a big bushy beard and J.V. Mackenzie's got wiry sideburns.

J.K.

J.V.M.

My staff are all excited and are even betting which hair will last longest without burning.

A few hours later...

Mackenzie's hair is still producing light! Hold on - looks like the electric current's been turned down and the bulb's too dim to be any use. RATS, I figure someone cheated to win the bets. I can't stand these failures - I should never have allowed the papers to print all that rubbish. Maybe I'll never solve this puzzle and go down in history as a dim failure.

DIM!

DIM!

17 October 1879

I was sitting in the office last night when a bright light bulb seemed to flash in my head. "Oh no - not another light bulb!" I moaned. Then I realized I was having A BRAINWAVE - that's what I mean by INSPIRATION. I thought burnt cotton thread that's turned to carbon might be the answer. Yeah - the magic material has to be carbon. After all, carbon only melts at really high temperatures of about 3500°C (6332°F). And now I've taken delivery of better air pumps the carbon shouldn't burn up. And ... well, I just have a hunch about cotton thread.

BUT WILL IT WORK??????

21 October 1879

I could cry. I've been working non-stop for days trying to make a cotton thread filament. Each one takes hours. But they keep breaking at the last moment. They're so thin and fragile. Oh well, here's number three. My heart's in my mouth and I'm switching on the new light bulb. It's burning . . . but for how long?

Keep burning . . . please.

Gnash!

cHEW!

← No 3

22 October 1879

It carried on burning. And burning. I didn't sleep last night. I watched it for every minute of the 13 hours and 30 minutes it stayed alight.

It works! I've done it. I'VE DONE IT!

I could weep with excitement and if I was a bit younger I'd be turning cartwheels. I've cracked the light bulb! No, not cracked the glass - I mean cracked the problem of how to make the light bulb stay alight. After 5,999 failures. YES!

NOW FOR A BLAZE OF PUBLICITY!!!

84

THE DAILY SUN

31 December 1879

Blaze of glory!

Heroic inventor Thomas A. Edison glowed with pride as he showed off his new invention.

Thousands of people watched him light up the whole town with 3,000 newly-invented light bulbs. Each one looks like a globe of sunshine. No more will people huddle in the dark afraid of the shadows. Thomas Edison is a shining example to the whole nation! It's such a pity that 14 of the new light bulbs have already been pinched.

---

1 January 1880

Terrible news. I've read that a British inventor Joseph Swan claims he invented the light bulb. And he's using carbon fibres just like me. I'm gnashing my teeth in rage. He says he's been working on it for 25 years. A likely story. He must be an impostor so I'll sue him in the courts for taking my invention. That's what I'll do – yep sue the pants off of 'him!

my bulb

Swan's blasted bulb

J.S.

But the British courts found that Swan had indeed been making light bulbs before Edison. Swan was a talented chemist whose inventions included artificial silk. He had finally made a successful carbon filament bulb in February 1879. But he didn't patent the invention because he thought people would copy it anyway.

If you were Thomas Edison what would you do next?

a) Pay Swan $1,000,000 to stop making light bulbs.

b) Try to sell cheaper light bulbs than Swan and drive him out of business.

c) Offer to join forces with Swan.

TEST YOUR TEACHER

Here's your chance to put your teacher under the spotlight. Ask them who invented the light bulb. If they know anything they'll say either Thomas Edison or Joseph Swan – or even both. Shake your head sadly and say:

As so often happens in science, the answer gets more complicated the more you find out. Several inventors made carbon filament lights before Swan and Edison. For example, Scottish inventor James Bowman Lindsay made one in 1835. But he didn't tell many people about it. Apparently, he didn't think there would be money in the new invention. And anyway, scientists have continued to improve on Edison's original design. Yes, it really does take quite a few scientists to invent a light bulb...

A BRIGHTER IDEA

A modern light bulb uses a coiled tungsten metal filament surrounded by argon – a harmless gas found in the air.

Modern heat resistant tungsten wires were developed by American William D. Coolidge (1873–1975) (yes, he really did live to 102). The idea of using a gas in the bulb came from another American, Irving Langmuir (1881–1957).

Bet you never knew!
Light bulbs save lives. Nowadays many lighthouses use electric light from powerful bulbs to warn ships away from rocks. Each lighthouse has its own pattern of flashes so that sailors can work out where they are in the dark.

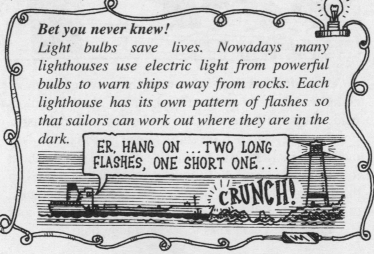

Of course, you'll find bulbs in lots of other places – you might even own a few yourself. Like in your bike lights or your torch.

Take a closer look at any of them and you'll find another amazing light gadget. What is it? A mirror of course, and it's there to reflect the light from the bulb outwards in the direction you want it to go in. And oddly enough, you'll find quite a few mirrors in the next frightening chapter.

FRIGHTENING REFLECTIONS

What's hard, and so shiny you can see your face in it?

No, it's NOT your teacher's bald head.

It's a mirror. When light hits a mirror an amazing thing happens. Light seems to bounce off it to form an image that we call a reflection. Oh, so you knew that already? Well, get this – reflections are unbelievably vital for light science. And they pop up in the most unlikely places.

Why not reflect on this quiz for a moment?

SPOT THE REFLECTION QUIZ

Reflections can help...

1 Road signs glow in the dark. TRUE/FALSE

2 Clouds glow in the sky. TRUE/FALSE

3 A TV set show pictures. TRUE/FALSE

4 A shellfish see. TRUE/FALSE

5 A doctor peer inside your eyeball. TRUE/FALSE

6 A mirage appear. TRUE/FALSE

7 Astronomers detect a black hole in space. TRUE/FALSE

8 The snow blind you. TRUE/FALSE

9 A surgeon peer inside your body without cutting you open. TRUE/FALSE

1 TRUE. You can find tiny mirrors in road signs and in road studs. The mirrors reflect car headlights. **2 TRUE.** Clouds reflect sunlight. That's what makes them bright and glowing. Thunderclouds appear dark and gloomy from the ground because they are thicker than ordinary clouds and reflect most of the sunlight upwards. Clouds that glow at night do so because they are high enough in the sky to still catch the sunlight. **3 FALSE.** There are no mirrors inside a TV set. **4 TRUE.** Scallops are a type of shellfish with tiny mirrors in their eyes. Each eye has a shiny layer of crystals that reflect light on to cells inside the eye. A scientist made this discovery whilst looking down a microscope at the shellfish. He saw his own face reflected in the creature's 100 gruesome eyes. **5 TRUE.** A doctor uses an ophthalmoscope (op-that-mo-scope) to peer inside your eyeball. This instrument shines a light on to a curved mirror that focuses the light beam into your eyeball. The doctor then peers through a hole in the middle of the mirror to inspect your nerves and blood vessels. **6 FALSE.** Mirages are caused by refraction. (Just to remind you, refraction is bended light.) **7 FALSE.** Light can't escape from a black hole (that's why they're black). So you can't spot one with a mirror. **8 TRUE.** Snow reflects light so well that you can be blinded by staring at it for too long in bright sunlight. That's why skiers wear protective goggles. **9 TRUE.** The tube is called an endoscope and it's basically two bundles of optical fibres. One bundle takes light from a light source at one end into the body – just imagine sticking a torch down your throat. The surgeon looks through the other bundle to get a close-up of your innards. And talking about optical fibres...

All right, this is what reflections can do. But how do you make reflections to begin with?

Frightening light fact file

NAME: Mirrors and reflections

THE BASIC FACTS: 1. A mirror is a piece of glass or transparent plastic with a silver backing.

2. A reflection happens like this. . .

PHOTONS OF LIGHT PASS THROUGH THE GLASS

OBJECT

REFLECTED OBJECT

VERY FEW LIGHT PHOTONS ARE SOAKED UP BY THE ATOMS OF THE SHINY SILVER BACKING. MOST BOUNCE OFF AGAIN TO FORM A REFLECTION

EYE

MIRROR

SILVER

THE FRIGHTENING DETAILS: Mirrors have a long and frightening history . . . as you're about to discover.

MURDEROUS MIRRORS

• Early people realized that shiny surfaces were great for seeing yourself in. Very handy for helping you brush your hair properly or spot an embarrassing bogie in your nostril.

• In ancient Egypt all sorts of things were used as mirrors including polished metal, wet slates and bowls of water. But none of them was smooth enough to give a clear, bright image. (In order to see your reflection you need a smooth surface so the photons reflect back together – remember?)

• By the time the Romans came along mirrors were much improved. The Romans used glass to make mirrors with a thin backing of tin. Unfortunately, this invention was to cause a few heated moments. According to legend the Greek scientist Archimedes (287–212 BC) used a bank of mirrors to burn Roman ships that were attacking his home city.

Every mirror reflected sunlight on to a single point on the ship. The wood heated up and burst into flames. This is scientifically possible although there's no proof it happened.

• In the Middle Ages Venice made the finest mirrors in the world. Venetians had learnt to use a mixture of mercury and tin for the backing which was easy to work without heating. This mixture was top secret. A special island was set aside for this work but the mercury was poisonous and many workers died or were driven mad by it. Nevertheless, they were forbidden to pass on the secret on pain of death.

• Somehow by the 1670s the secret had spread to France and then across Europe. In 1840, German chemist, Justus von Liebig (1803–1873) found how to put silver backing on a mirror using heated silver nitrate and other chemicals. And this method is still in use.

• Meanwhile the Chinese had been making excellent mirrors from polished metal for over 2,000 years. Some of these mirrors were called "magic mirrors". Can you solve the riddle of their amazing powers?

COULD YOU BE A SCIENTIST?

You shine a light on a magic mirror. The polished bronze surface reflects back the light on the screen together with a pattern.

But there is no pattern on the surface of the mirror itself. So what causes this strange effect? Only the makers knew the secret. Western and Chinese scientists had been baffled for years. Some Chinese thinkers believed that there was an invisible pattern etched on the front of the mirror that showed up in the reflection.

How would you explain the mirrors?

a) The Chinese thinkers were right. There was a faint pattern on the mirror's surface.

b) The mirrors gave out X-rays that revealed a hidden pattern under the surface.

c) There was a hidden pattern on the back of the mirror that was somehow being reflected from the front.

Answer:

c) The first westerners to find the answer were two British physicists, W.E. Ayrton and J. Perry. In the 1890s they were allowed to visit workshops where the mirrors were made.

1 A PATTERN IS ENGRAVED ON THE BACK OF THE MIRROR

2 THE FRONT SURFACE IS A LAYER OF METAL THAT HAS BEEN SCRAPED UNTIL IT'S VERY THIN

3 LIGHT REFLECTS OFF THE PARTS OF THE SURFACE COVERING THE PATTERN AT A SLIGHTLY DIFFERENT ANGLE TO THE REST OF THE MIRROR

4 THIS CAUSES THE PATTERN TO APPEAR AS DARK LINES ON THE SCREEN

SO WHAT'RE YOU SMILING AT?

The pattern appears as dark lines on the screen.

Bet you never knew!
In the Middle Ages people believed they could see the future by staring at a shiny surface such as a mirror. This practice was known as scrying (sk-ry-ing) – it's the origin of the traditional fortune teller's crystal ball. Other shiny surfaces used were bowls of water or blood.

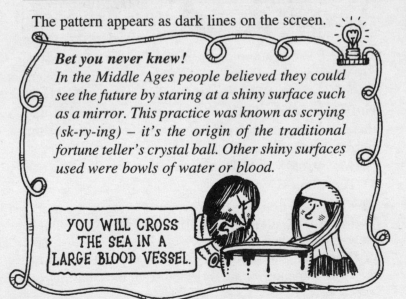

YOU WILL CROSS THE SEA IN A LARGE BLOOD VESSEL.

And talking about the bad old days...

TEACHER'S TEA-BREAK TEASER

When your grandparents were young, cruel parents and teachers sometimes forced children to shine their shoes until they could see their faces in them. Here's your chance to get a belated revenge. Knock politely on the staffroom door. When it grinds open smile sweetly and enquire...

Note: there's no point in showing your teacher a pair of smelly trainers. Ideally you should be holding a nice pair of shiny shoes for their inspection.

SHINY SHOES   SMELLY TRAINERS

Answer:
Like any non-shiny object, leather is naturally bumpy and reflects light in all directions. That's why you can't see a clear reflection in it. The polish fills in the tiny dips in the leather to make a nice smooth surface that reflects light well and looks jolly smart.

Dare you discover ... what a mirror does to light?

You will need:
A mirror
Two eyebrows and yourself

What you do:
1 Stand in front of the mirror.
2 Raise your left eyebrow. (If you
can't do this just point to your left eyebrow instead.)

What does your reflection do?
a) It raises its left eyebrow.
b) The reflection raises its right eyebrow.
c) The reflection raises its right eyebrow but there's a delay of about half a second.

One of the first scientists to investigate reflection was born long ago in what is now Iraq. Europeans call him Alhazen but his proper name was Abu al-Hassan ibn al-Haytham. Here's his story...

Hall of fame: Ibn al-Haytham (965–1040)
Nationality: Arab

Although he was a great scientist al-Haytham was unlucky enough to serve a mad ruler – Egyptian Caliph al-Hakim (985–1021).

According to an old story, one day the scientist boasted to the Caliph that he could build a dam across the River Nile. Big mistake. The Caliph sent al-Haytham to southern Egypt but there he realized there was no suitable site for the dam. There were too many waterfalls. When al-Haytham returned to admit failure the Caliph was furious. He made the scientist stand on a bench and he had the bench hacked to pieces. The Caliph made it horribly clear that al-Haytham was lucky not to be hacked to pieces himself.

The Caliph gave al-Haytham an obscure government job. But the Caliph was not a man to cross and the scientist decided on a plan to save his life. He pretended to go mad. Al-Haytham was locked up and the Caliph forgot to have him killed. Ironically, a few years later the Caliph went mad himself and was murdered by an unknown hand. Afterwards al-Haytham told everyone that he had just been pretending.

THE BORING TRUTH?

Of course, some boring historians say this is a story that people told after the scientist's death. Al-Haytham never mentioned it in any of his writings. But then why should he? He'd probably have wanted to forget the incident. And why should he risk raking up the past? What do you think?

The scientist got a job teaching at the Azhar mosque and copying ancient Greek manuscripts. And there he became interested in light. So he wrote a book called *The Treasury of Optics* in which he described his brilliant discoveries. (Unfortunately, he didn't describe his experiments in any detail.)

The Treasury of Optics
by Ibn al-Haytham

I'm not one to boast but I'm forced to admit that I am a brilliant scientist. I have found secrets about light that no one has ever discovered before. And what's more, I have proved all this by mathematical calculations and through experiments using mirrors that I made with my very own hands.

1. Light is given out by glowing objects. Some of the ancient Greek writers believed that light came from the eye and it was this that made the object glow. But I, Ibn al-Haytham have proved them all wrong!

2. Light travels in a straight line. Now as I said, I'm not one to blow my own trumpet - but this was one of my most ingenious and clever experiments. I made a hole in my wall so that the shaft of light entered the room. Then I checked the shaft of light and found it was perfectly straight. Brilliant!

3. Light always reflects at a predictable angle. By the most careful and painstaking measurements worthy only of the highest genius I have proved that if light shines from the left of a mirror it will bounce off to the right or vice-versa. And always at the same mathematically predictable angle.

Object

Reflected object

Eye

Mirror

Angle the same but opposite

Although I'm really a very humble, modest person I am sure the name of Ibn al-Haytham will live for ever in history and all the world will want to read of my discoveries!

But people elsewhere in the world weren't interested in light and it took 200 years for al-Haytham's book to even appear in the West. Could you be a scientist like al-Haytham and discover the secrets of reflections? Here's your chance...

Dare you discover ... how mirrors can change your appearance?

You will need:
A shiny tablespoon

What you do:
1 Hold the spoon like a hand mirror.
2 Look in the back of the spoon and then the front.

What do you notice?
a) My face appears upside-down in the back of the spoon and the right way up in the front.
b) My face appears fatter in the back of the spoon and upside-down with a long neck in the front of the spoon.
c) My face appears normal in the back of the spoon. In the front of the spoon I'm the right way up but I have a huge hooter.

Answer:
b) The front of the spoon is concave – that is it curves inwards at the centre. (To remember this word just imagine a cave shaped in the same way.)

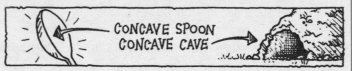

CONCAVE SPOON
CONCAVE CAVE

Because of this shape, light reflecting from your face reflects downwards from the top of the spoon and upwards from the bottom.

You see the bottom of your face at the top of the spoon and the top at the bottom. And your face appears upside-down. Turn the spoon around and you're faced with a bulging or as scientists say a convex shape.

BULGING CENTRE
BULGING TUMMY

CONVEX MIRROR

CONVEX SCIENTIST

The convex shape reflects the light from your face and spreads it slightly outwards. This makes your face appear rounder and fatter (though ths time you're the right way up!).

HORRIBLE HEALTH WARNING!

Your parents may not appreciate you performing this interesting experiment at meal times. Especially when the posh relatives are waiting for their brussels sprouts and you're using the best silver tablespoon.

Dare you discover ... how to make a ghost appear?

(This experiment is so good you'll want to do it again and again. All in the interests of Science, of course.)

You will need:

Sticky tape
Scissors
A small but bright torch
A mirror – about 24 cm x 36 cm is ideal.
A piece of black paper (larger than your mirror).
A pencil
A large black water-based felt-tip marker.
A room with light-coloured walls.

What you do:

1 Draw the outline of your ghost on the black paper. This should be smaller than the mirror.

2 Cut out the outline.

3 Stick the remaining paper with the ghost shape removed over the mirror.

4 Use the felt tip to draw in the features of your ghost in the ghost shape on the mirror.

5 Darken the room. Better still wait until nightfall – after all, that's when ghosts appear.

IS NOW OK?

SURE!

6 Prop the mirror securely on an arm chair. The mirror should be facing the wall about two metres away. Shine your torch at the mirror. Your ghost appears on the wall.

7 Move the torch so the ghost appears to float in the air.

WHOOOOOOOO!*

WALL

*SUGGESTED NOISE FOR ADDED EFFECT

What is the scientific explanation for the ghost?
a) The torch light reflects off the black paper and the felt tip lines.
b) The light reflects off the mirror but not the paper or the lines.
c) The light reflects off everything.

HORRIBLE HEALTH WARNING!

1 Don't try this experiment until you've checked with your parents it's OK to draw on the mirror. Defacing your granny's priceless antique mirror could prove fatal.

2 Be careful when handling the mirror. Mirrors are glass (surprise, surprise) and they can break and injure people. And give you seven years bad luck, so it's said.

> DRAT! I HAVEN'T BROKEN A MIRROR FOR SIX YEARS, ELEVEN MONTHS AND THIRTY DAYS

SMASH!

> CRIKEY, THAT'S BAD LUCK, THEN!

3 Make sure the felt-tip pen is water based. It should be possible to wipe the ink off with water.

Whilst we're talking about frightening things, I should warn you about the next chapter. Beware – lurking among the weird facts in the chapter is a sinister-looking spider.

Will it frighten the socks off you? Read on and find out...

ARGH!

FRIGHTENING LIGHT-BENDERS

What have all these things got in common?

Yes, I know they all contain glass but that *isn't* the only CORRECT answer. Give up? Well, the other answer is that they all bend or refract light. But how do they do it?

Well, bend your eyes to this...

Frightening light fact file

NAME: Refraction

THE BASIC FACTS: Light bends when it passes at an angle from one transparent (see-through) substance to another. Like this...

THE FRIGHTENING DETAILS: Refraction can cause some horrible accidents (see page 109). But first...

Here's a slow-motion replay of refraction as light hits that fish tank.

LIGHT BEAM HITS THE WATER AT AN ANGLE

THE PHOTONS PUSH THEIR WAY PAST THE ATOMS IN THE WATER. WITH ALL THIS HASSLE, THE LIGHT PHOTONS LOSE ABOUT ONE THIRD OF THEIR SPEED

45°

PHOTONS ON THIS SIDE SLOW DOWN FIRST AS THEY HIT THE WATER →

THIS BENDS THE BEAM

HMMM, I FANCY A 'LIGHT' SNACK

HORRIBLE REFRACTION ACCIDENTS

1 Ever stared straight down into a swimming pool and wondered how deep it is? Well, it's deeper than you think. Refraction bends light reflecting from the bottom of the pool. So it appears closer.

I'M JUST GOING FOR A PADDLE, MUM. . .

2 Told you...

3 You can see this effect if you stare down at your legs in the water. They appear stumpy and short. It's true – honest, I'm not pulling your leg.

4 In South America, and parts of the Pacific and Africa people fish with spears but thanks to refraction the fish often get away. And accidents do happen...

DISAPPEARING ACTS

But refraction can do even weirder things. Like making objects disappear. Oh, so you don't believe me, well, try this...

Dare you discover ... how to make a coin disappear?

You will need:
A £1 coin
A wash basin
A ruler

What you do:

1 Fill the basin with water to a depth of 4 cm.
2 Place the coin in the water.

3 Crouch down so that you can just see the coin over the rim of the wash basin.

4 Lift the plug slightly so the water level in the sink falls slowly.

As the water drains down the plug hole the coin gradually disappears. *Why?*

a) Grrrr! My coin has gone down the drain!

b) The water refracted the light reflecting back from the coin so it made the coin look further away than it really was.

c) The light from the coin was refracted so the coin appeared closer.

Answer:
c) The water bent the light towards you so the coin appeared closer. As the water drained away the light refracted less. The coin appeared to move away until it disappeared behind the rim. But actually the coin didn't move.

If refraction can make coins vanish then maybe it can make a larger object disappear. Perhaps even a human being? Here's a story in which this happens – but is it true? What do you think?

Now you see me, now you don't

LONDON, 1897

Tonight I became invisible. As I watched my own body disappear I remembered how hard I worked under cover of darkness so no one could steal my ideas. All those years of frustration and poverty and disappointment. Now, at last I have succeeded.

It was a strange, frightening experience. First I took drugs for several days to remove all the colour pigments from my body. My skin and hair turned snow white. (Even now the side-effects cause me pain.) Then I stood between two electrical power sources. These make the strange invisible rays that I have discovered. Rays that alter the atoms of water in my body so they no longer refract light. In this way, light shines straight through my body as if I were made of air.

As the rays fell on my body I felt I was becoming a ghost. My white face and hair slowly grew dimmer until I could see nothing

112

in the mirror. The skin of my arms and legs looked like glass – I could see the fat and nerves beneath.

And gradually everything faded away until I could stand before the mirror and see nothing but an empty room. . .

Answer:
Great story, isn't it? It's based on *The Invisible Man* by H.G. Wells (1866–1946). But it's only a story because: 1 The rays described don't exist. 2 If the scientist had no pigments then he wouldn't have pigments in his retina to help him see. 3 The lens and cornea of the eye refract light and focus it on to the retina. (Remember that bit from page 45?) But if the scientist's invisible body didn't refract light then these bits of his eye wouldn't refract it either. So he couldn't see the room.

BRILLIANT LENSES

Assuming you're not invisible, lenses are a brilliant way to refract light. They come in two main varieties, convex and concave. (Remember these words?)

CONVEX LENS LIGHT BENDS INWARDS

CONCAVE LENS LIGHT BENDS OUTWARDS

CONVICT LEN BENDS BARS

OK, let's take a peek through these lenses. And here's a particularly revolting hairy spider to study...

1 Through a convex lens the spider appears bigger. Let's take a look at the spider's head.

2 Light reflects off the spider's ugly little mug.

The convex lens bends this light towards a single point.

3 If you put your eye at this point you'll see a close-up view of the spider's head with eight huge beady eyes staring back at you. YIKES!

Let's use a concave lens to take another look at the spider. Yes, it's all in the interests of Science.

1 This lens spreads the light wider.

2 And when you look through the lens the spider appears much smaller. Phew! Not so bad – eh?

So concave lenses make things look smaller and convex lenses make them look bigger. And not surprisingly you find convex lenses in cameras, binoculars, telescopes, microscopes and loads of scientific instruments which make things appear larger.

Of course, if you're wearing glasses to read this page you'll know all about lenses. You've got two of them perched on the end of your nose. But why wear them?

FRIGHTENING EXPRESSIONS

An ophthalmologist says...

YOU MAY HAVE HYPEROPIA, MYOPIA OR ASTIGMATISM

Are any of these fatal?

Answer:

No, they're eye problems caused by faulty focusing.

1 **Hyperopia** (hi-per-rop-pia) means that you're long-sighted. The lens of your eye doesn't bend light enough. This means that it can't focus light from close objects on to your retina. So close up objects look blurred. A similar effect can be caused if your eyeball is too short.

2 **Myopia** (mi-ope-ia) is short-sightedness. That's when the light reflecting from a distant object gets bent too far by your lens and distant objects seem blurred. A similar effect can be caused if your eyeball is too long.

3 **Astigmatism** (as-stig-ma-tism) is when the cornea is slightly out of shape. This results in part of the image appearing blurred.

If you've got any of these you'll need to wear glasses or contact lenses to correct the problem. Cheer up you'll look dead brainy and they're scientifically fascinating...

SPECTACULAR SPECTACLES

1 The first glasses to be invented had convex lenses. They were probably invented in Italy in the thirteenth century and worn by long-sighted people.

2 As you've just discovered, the long-sighted eye has a lens that doesn't bend the light inwards enough to focus an image on the retina.

A convex lens bends the light further inwards to focus an image.

3 Concave lenses were first made in around 1451. German churchman Nicholas of Cusa (1401–1464) worked out that this shape could help short-sighted people. What a far-sighted man!

4 A short-sighted eye lens pushes the light inwards too much. So the light focuses before it gets to the retina.

The concave lens spreads the light so it focuses on the retina.

5 Contact lenses do the same job as glasses. Nowadays they're slices of soft watery plastic that fit over the eyeball. But the first lenses invented by German Adolf Fick (1829–1901) in 1888 were made of glass. The glass rubbed against the eyeballs and made them sore. What a sight for sore eyes!

6 And Adolf even managed to make lenses of exactly the right shape to fit over the eyeball and bend light on to the retina. The answer was to shape the lenses in moulds made by using the eyeballs of dead people.

7 DON'T WORRY! Your local optician DOESN'T have a drawer full of eyeballs. Nowadays, they measure the curve of your eyeballs using a keratometer (ker-rato-meter). This instrument directs a beam of light into your eyeball (which reflects it) and records the position of the reflected light. This data is used to calculate its exact curve.

8 Not surprisingly, it was a pair of spectacle makers who found a new use for their lenses. In 1608 Dutch spectacle maker, Hans Lippershey (1570–1618) invented the telescope and soon afterwards his assistant Zacharius Jannsen (1580–1638) invented the microscope. Or did they?

Hans Lippershey got the idea for the telescope after watching two children playing with his lenses. The children placed two convex lenses at a distance and they found they could see their local church steeple in amazing detail. Apparently neither Hans nor anyone else had tried this experiment. The Dutch government gave Hans 900 florins for his invention but the poor children didn't get a peek at the money (not even through a telescope).

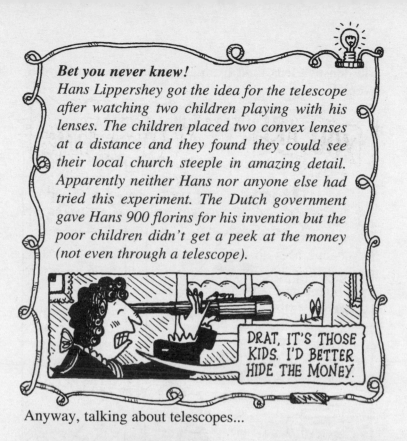

DRAT, IT'S THOSE KIDS. I'D BETTER HIDE THE MONEY.

Anyway, talking about telescopes...

FRIGHTENING EXPRESSIONS...

ARGH! IT'S CHROMATIC ABERRATION!

Sounds frightening. Could this mean the end of the world? No. Chromatic aberration means he's got a problem with his telescope. It's caused by different-size light waves being refracted by different amounts.

A traditional telescope has two or more convex lenses.

119

The lenses focus light from a distant object on to your eyeball.

THERE'S A HUMANOID WATCHING US, HE'S GOT A VERY LONG NOSE!

LENS **1** CONCENTRATES THE LIGHT FROM A DISTANT OBJECT TO FORM AN IMAGE

LENS **2** TURNS THE IMAGE THE RIGHT WAY UP

LENS **3** FOCUSES THE IMAGE ONTO THE WATCHER'S EYE

4 THE EYE LENS FOCUSES THE IMAGE ONTO THE RETINA

But here's the problem. Because different coloured lights refract at different angles, they don't all focus in exactly the same spot. So images would have a coloured "halo" around the edge – and that's chromatic aberration.

Luckily for astronomers, Isaac Newton solved this problem in 1668. He designed a telescope that used a concave mirror to focus the light instead of a lens.

Because mirrors reflect all wavelengths in the same way, there was no "halo" around the image. And Newton's design is still in use today.

Bet you never knew!
Telescopes aren't just for watching the stars or seeing things in the distance. You'll also find a telescope in a scientific instrument called a spectroscope.

SUBSTANCE TO BE STUDIED GOES IN HERE AND HAS A BRIGHT LIGHT SHONE ON IT

A PRISM BREAKS THE LIGHT INTO COLOURS

WOW!

LIGHT REFLECTS OFF THE SUBSTANCE YOU ARE OBSERVING

THE TELESCOPE ALLOWS A SCIENTIST TO GET A CLOSE LOOK AT THE COLOURS

Talking of colours you'd better read the next chapter. It's full of crucial colourful facts. Yep, colour is CRUCIAL – I mean, where would drivers be if they couldn't tell the difference between a green and a red light? In hospital that's where!

Well, you've got the green light to turn over the page.

READY STEADY TURN!

CRUCIAL COLOUR

Life without colour would be frighteningly boring. Just like an endless awful, old black and white movie. Without colour you'd never get to enjoy the glory of a peacock's tail, a glowing sunset or a garden full of flowers.

Mind you, you wouldn't have to shudder at the frightening crimson, purple and brown decor in your auntie's living room.

A NOTE TO THE READER

We apologize for the loss of colour. Readers will have to imagine the wonderful glowing, vibrant colours described in these pages. And if you do get bored you can always colour them in.
PS If it's not your book go and buy your own before you pick up your crayons. Anyway, here's how light makes colour appear.

Frightening light fact file

NAME: Colours

THE BASIC FACTS: **1.** White light is a muddled-up mix of all the colours of the rainbow and each colour is made of a light wave with a different frequency (energy level). Remember all that?

2. When light hits an object some of the colours are soaked up and others are reflected. And it's the reflected colours that we see. Got all that?

THE FRIGHTENING DETAILS: When something is black all the colours in light are soaked up so nothing reflects back. This explains the colour of this big black revolting slug.

YEAH, CHEERS!

Read on for more colourful facts.

THE COLOURFUL FACTS

A green leaf or caterpillar soaks up all the colours in light except green. Green reflects off the leaf (or caterpillar) and that's what you see.

GARDENER'S GREEN FINGERS

GREEN PLANT

GREEN CATERPILLAR

A ripe tomato soaks up all kinds of light except red.

White objects reflect every kind of light. (Don't forget white light is all the colours mixed up.)

POLAR BEAR IN THE SNOW (WEARING A WHITE BOBBLE HAT).

Bet you never knew!
1 *Windows, polythene bags and bottles don't reflect colours. They're see-through or "transparent" as a scientist would say. With a see-through material, such as glass, the atoms form thin layers or are regularly spaced so most light gets through. That's how light manages to shine through your window – it's transparently obvious.*
2 *Some fish are transparent. For example, the X-ray fish, found in South American rivers has no pigments. This allows it to hide from attackers. The fish is a bit like the Invisible Man on page 112 except you can see its skeleton and guts through the skin.*

I ADMIRE YOUR GUTS

YOURS LOOK PRETTY COOL, TOO!

Dare you discover ... where colour comes from?

You will need:
A nice juicy red tomato
A piece of white A4 paper
A small but bright torch

What you do:
1 Darken the room or better still wait for nightfall.
2 Place the tomato on one end of the paper.
3 Hold the torch over the paper level with the tomato. Shine the light on the tomato.

4 Look at the area of shadow under the torch beam. It should be glowing pink. *Why?*
a) The tomato is reflecting red light on to the paper.
b) It's a trick of my eyes caused by the torch light.
c) The shadow of the tomato is soaking up all the colours in light except red.

Answer:
a) White paper reflects all the colours of light that fall on it. The pink glow is due to the red light reflecting off the tomato and on to the paper. All the other colours in the light get soaked up by the tomato. The experiment proves that colours are indeed caused by the reflection of light.

Most objects, though, reflect a mix of different coloured light. Take bananas, for example....

TEACHER'S TEA-BREAK TEASER

You will need a banana and a lot of courage. Rap smartly on the staffroom door. When it squeaks open put on your most innocent expression and enquire...

Answer:
Well, it might appear yellow but it actually reflects red and green light and soaks up blue light. Your eyes see this mix of red and green as yellow. (You can find out how on pages 134-135.)

Bet you never knew!
Is your street lit by sodium lights? (These are the bright orange lights.) In this light (provided there are no other types of light near by) red things such as lipstick, blood or geraniums appear black. Sodium light contains no red light. Because red objects can't reflect any red light you see them as black.

WE'RE GOING TO A DISCO NOT A FUNERAL

WHY ARE YOU WEARING BLACK LIPSTICK, THEN?

Talking about reflecting colours, did you know two scientists spent their holidays reflecting on this very topic? That's sad.

Hall of fame: Chandrasekhara Vankata Raman (1888–1970) Nationality: Indian
John Strutt, Lord Rayleigh (1824–1919) Nationality: British
You couldn't find two more different characters than C.V. Raman and John Strutt.

Raman was a brilliant scientist but he had to work for the Indian civil service as a young man because of a shortage of scientific jobs in India. (In 1917 he became Professor of Physics at Calcutta University.) Strutt was a rich lord with a private laboratory in his mansion and a top university job in England. They worked separately to solve two tricky light questions but by an odd coincidence Raman later became friendly with Strutt's son.

The questions sound childishly simple...

But these questions aren't stupid and the answers are frighteningly complicated ... as you're about to discover.

In 1871 John Strutt went on holiday to Egypt. Cruising through the Mediterranean, he admired the lovely blue sky and sea.

Being a scientist, though, he did more than enjoy what he saw. He used his scientific know-how to explain it. His letter home might have read like this...

To Lord & Lady Rayleigh,
Tering Place, Essex, England.

Dear Mum and Dad,
Having a great holiday! I've read lots
of science books and there's plenty
of interesting sights to fascinate a
budding scientist like me. Like the
blue sky and sea, for example. I
mean, what makes them so blue? I
suspect atoms in the air reflect
light. I think blue light is
scattered much better than other
lights (I'm not sure why) so we see
more of it. I reckon the sea is blue
because it reflects the sky.
  Oh, I forgot to say, the cruise is OK.
Yours scientifically,
John

NOTES TO THE READER...

1 John was right. Blue light photons have more energy and this makes them more likely to bounce off the atoms downwards and into our eyes. So we get to see more blue light photons when we look at the sky. And that makes the sky appear blue. Honest, it's a true-blue fact!.

2 But sunsets aren't blue – are they? Well, this actually proves John Strutt was right. When the sun is low we see its light shining at an angle through all the grotty old dust in the air. The dust reflects away most of the blue photons before the light gets to us. But who cares? We get to enjoy the reddish-orange colours that were in the sunlight and didn't get reflected upwards so much.

OK, now back to the story...

In 1921, Raman was sailing to a Science conference in Britain. Feeling rather bored he decided to test John Strutt's findings about the sea. By this time the older scientist was dead so Raman couldn't drop him a postcard. But he might have written to his pal John Strutt's scientist son, Robert Strutt, the next Lord Rayleigh (1875–1947).

To Robert Strutt (Lord Rayleigh), Tering Place, Essex, England.

Dear Bob,

Fab weather! Your old dad was right about the blue sky. But I don't think the sea is blue 'cause of the sky. I looked at the sea using a Nicol prism I had on me. As you know the atoms of the prism are arranged so that light from only one direction can get through. And get this – although the prism blocked light reflecting off the sea from the sky, the sea still glowed blue! The cause of the glow's got me baffled – but I'm glowing to find out. Ha ha. Keep you posted.

Your mate, C.V. Raman

So why *was* the sea blue?

Back at his lab in 1922 Raman did a series of experiments that involved shining light through water and found the answer...

Dear Bob,

I've cracked it. I was looking into why the sea is blue - remember? Well, here's what I've found out:

1. Part of the light from the sky is reflected by the surface of the sea. OK - your dad got that bit right. That's why the sea is grey when the sky is dark and cloudy. But lots of photons get into the sea itself...

blue sky

2. The seawater soaks up most of these photons and only reflects back blue light photons. This is the blue glow I saw.

blue photons

light photons

I'm sure your old dad would have been chuffed.

Your Pal,
C.V. Raman

blue glow

For Raman, it must have seemed that the sky (and the sea) was the limit. He went on to find how bonds between atoms in a chemical can affect an atom's wobble and add or remove energy from the reflecting photons. And in 1930 he won the Nobel Prize for this work.

MYSTERIOUS COLOUR MIXING

On their own, colours are fairly straightforward. But try mixing them together and the facts get murky.

Bet you never knew!
Colour photos are made by mixing different light colours.
1 The first colour picture was taken by Scottish physicist James Clerk Maxwell (1831–1879). In 1863 he took three snaps of one of his wife's ribbons. One through a red filter, one blue and one green. Each filter blocked all the colours in light except its particular colour. So the green filter, for example, showed up the green parts of the pattern. He combined the images to make a colour picture.

FASCINATING, CAN I HAVE IT BACK NOW?

2 Nowadays, though, colour films consist of three layers of chemicals. The top layer makes a blue colour from blue light, the second makes green in the same way and the third makes a red colour. Between them the chemicals build up an image. Our brains do the rest of the colour mixing – as you'll discover on pages 134-135.

MUDDY MIXED-UP PAINTS

But just imagine that you tried to make a painting in the same way as a photo. You carefully mixed thin layers of blue, green and red. And produced a muddy black smear.

I CALL THIS, "FLY'S VIEW OF A COWPAT"

Want to know why? Why not ask your art teacher...

TEST YOUR ART TEACHER

If you mix green and red and blue light together you'll get a pale whitish sort of a colour. But if you mix together green and red and blue paints you get black – why?

Answer:

White light is made up of all colours. So the more colours of light you mix the closer you get to white light. But paints and other coloured objects (like tomatoes and bananas) work by soaking up some light colours and reflecting others. So the more paints you add to your mix the closer you get to something that soaks up every colour in light. In other words – black.

YOU'VE ADDED MORE PAINT

YES. NOW IT'S CALLED, "BLACK CAT IN A POWERCUT"

CRUCIAL COLOUR VISION

Whatever colours you manage to mix you'll need a pair of eyes to appreciate them. Humans, birds and apes are lucky in this respect. We view the world in glorious living Technicolor. Unlike for example, a squid, which can only see black and white or your pet cat who sees green and blue and violet but not red. (Scientists aren't quite sure why this is – but when Tiddles finishes off a mouse she sees the blood and gory bits as green.)

HOW YOU SEE IN COLOUR

1 Unlike Tiddles you've actually got three types of cone cells in your retina – one each for green, blue and red light. All the colours you see are made from mixing at least two of these colours. (For more info. on mixing light see page 126.)

2 Your incredible eyes are able to make out up to ten million different colours. It's amazing to think they can do this from just three basic colours. Here's your chance to test this remarkable ability...

Dare you discover ... how you see colours?

You will need:

A piece of black paper

A small piece of yellow paper about 3 cm square.

Your head complete with eyeballs.

What you do:

1 Place the yellow paper on the black paper and stare at it for 30 seconds without moving your head or blinking.

2 You should see a square of blue appearing round the edge of the yellow square.

What do you notice?

a) The cells that fire blue signals take time to work – but now they've detected blue colouring in the black paper.

b) The yellow paper has excited your blue cells so much they've gone into overdrive. And now you're seeing too much blue.

c) The green and red cells that give you yellow are getting tired but the blue cells are still firing.

Answer:

c) Your eye sees yellow by firing green and red cone cells (remember the banana?). Your brain mixes these sensations to make yellow. But after a while the cells become less sensitive. Meanwhile blue cone cells are still firing in this area of your retina so you see a blue image. You see "after-images" for the same reason. Mind you – it took a few disgusting eyeball experiments before scientists worked this out...

EYEBALL TO EYEBALL

WARNING: DISGUSTING FACTS COMING UP. (Hopefully your breakfast won't be coming up after you read them.)

Isaac Newton reckoned we see colours by changing the shape of our eyeballs. Isaac thought this helped the eye to refract white light into coloured light that then fell on the retina.

To test this idea Isaac stuck what might have been a toothpick under his eyeball. A toothpick is a stick for getting bits of food out from between your teeth. Isaac's toothpick was probably encrusted with millions of germs and the stale remains of his supper. YUCK!

Using the toothpick Isaac squeezed his own eyeball to change its shape. He saw a few lights, but not enough to prove his theory.

The germs on the toothpick infected his eyeball. It became so painful that he had to go to bed for two weeks. This proves that even a scientific genius can do very stupid things.

MORE COLOURFUL SCIENTISTS...

After Newton, other famous scientists probed colour
vision. The story continues with British chemist John
Dalton (1766–1844). John Dalton was one of the first
people to suggest that there were such things as atoms.
But come to think of it, he wasn't too colourful himself.

A fellow scientist said:

HIS STYLE OF
WRITING AND
CONVERSATION
ARE DRY

Nowadays we might call him "boring". Boring John
loved to study flowers. Unfortunately, he found that he
couldn't see red colours properly...

IT'S
BLUE

IT'S
RED

NO NEED
TO GET
ALL BLUE
IN THE
FACE
ABOUT IT

John suffered from colour deficiency – a condition that
affects about one in 25 people and he enjoyed giving
boring lectures on the subject. According to John colour
deficiency was caused by a build up of blue juice in the
eyeball. The blue colour soaks up red light.

He made arrangements for his eyeballs to be removed after his death to check for blue juice.

IT WON'T MAKE A BLIND BIT OF DIFFERENCE TO ME IF I'M DEAD

Meanwhile our old pal Thomas Young had been treating patients with colour deficiency. As a result of this work he believed the retina had separate regions that detected red, blue and violet. And Dalton had a problem with his red region.

Unfortunately Young died before Dalton's eyeballs were removed so he never knew the result. In fact, the jelly in Dalton's eyeballs proved to be nice and clear. Dalton would have been dead disappointed if he wasn't already dead.

OH WELL, YOU MIGHT AS WELL POP THEM BACK IN HIS HEAD

EYE EYE, SIR!

THE MYSTERY SOLVED...

The mystery was solved by another famous scientist, James Clerk Maxwell. He spun a disc divided into green and red and blue sections. The colours appeared to merge into white. People who couldn't see the colour red saw white in a spinning disc that had only blue and green sections. This proved...

1 That the cone cells in our eyes can see green, blue and red light.

2 That they make all the other colours from these three. (The white colour was a mix of all the other colours.)

3 In colour deficient people one type of cone cell is missing or not working properly.

Bet you never knew!
As long as your vision's working OK you're bound to enjoy a multi-coloured laser show. By using different chemicals in lasers scientists can change the colour of this light. For example, atoms of ruby produce red light. But you can't enjoy the pretty colours by gazing directly into a laser beam. It's so bright it would probably blind you or heat up your eyeball until it boils.

Dare you take a closer look at lasers? Why not turn to the next frightening chapter?

BLISTERING LASERS

As you're about to find out, lasers are a huge part of modern life and they're set to brighten up our future too. Like all great inventions, lasers began with a flash of inspiration.

A LASER FLASH OF INSPIRATION
In 1951 US scientist Charles H. Townes was at a scientific conference in Washington.

I'M TRYING TO PRODUCE HIGH-POWERED RADIO WAVES THAT CAN BE USED TO STUDY THE STRUCTURE OF ATOMS

FASCINATING!

That night Townes couldn't sleep. His mind was working overtime on the problem. So very early the next morning before it got light he went for a walk and ended up on a park bench. He was looking for inspiration.

THINK! THINK!

Suddenly he found it. Townes scribbled his ideas on the back of an old envelope. If you could control the speed the atoms wobble and stop the light escaping you could create a powerful beam of light. Since radio waves are made by photons you could do the same things with radio waves.

1. Heat up atoms (Better find the right atoms to use.)

2. Heated-up atoms give out radio waves.

3. Stop the radio waves escaping until they form a high-powered beam.

Townes later found out he had been sitting opposite of the house of famous inventor Alexander Graham Bell (1847–1922). And Townes wondered if the dead inventor had provided ghostly assistance.

Later Townes realized that you could use light instead of radio waves. By 1958 working with his brother-in-law, Arthur Schawlow, Townes had worked out how a laser might work. He even coined the name "laser" over lunch. But he had little idea of how useful the laser would become. He later said:

IT WAS BY NO MEANS CLEAR . . . THAT (THE LASER) WOULD SEE SO MANY STRIKING APPLICATIONS.

For scientists at the time, building a laser just seemed a fascinating technical challenge.

In 1960 another US physicist, Theodore Maiman used Townes's plans to build the world's first working laser.

In 1964 Townes won the Nobel Prize for his work together with two Russian scientists, Nikolai Basov and Alexander Prokhorov who developed the laser separately but at the same time.

Interesting postscript:
Actually, unknown to Townes, the idea of a laser and perhaps even the name had been dreamt up by another US scientist, Gordon Gould in 1957. Unfortunately, Gould didn't publish his idea and he didn't take out a patent in time so he missed out on the glory.

LASER DEFENCE SYSTEMS

Lasers have loads of uses. One purpose developed by the US military is a laser defence system to shoot down enemy missiles. Sounds exciting? Well, here's how to defend your school from hostile attack with a laser defence system.

HORRIBLE HEALTH WARNINGS!

1 Laser beams can sizzle human flesh. Do not direct your laser beam anywhere near a teacher or any other poor defenceless creatures.

2 This laser is highly destructive. You can only read this section if you promise to use your laser system to PROTECT your school. And NOT to vaporize the buildings before science class on Monday.

HOW TO MAKE YOUR OWN LASER DEFENCE SYSTEM

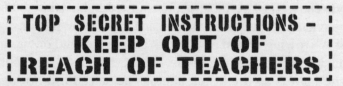

TOP SECRET INSTRUCTIONS – KEEP OUT OF REACH OF TEACHERS

Step 1 – assemble your materials.

To build your own laser defence system you will need...

A power supply.

A box lined with mirrors. Leave a partly-silvered mirror in one end for your laser to shine through.

Something to produce light photons (a block of ruby will do).

A bucket of water.

You will also need...

A high-speed jet plane complete with pilot and a

computer controlled high sensitivity heat detecting system. (You may be able to borrow these from your local air force base.)

NO PROBLEM. SON. DROP IT BACK AROUND TEA-TIME

Step 2 – assemble your laser.

1 Place the ruby in the box and link it up to your power supply.

MIRRORS RUBY

POWER SUPPLY

ENEMY AIRCRAFT SPOTTED OVER JUNIOR PLAYING FIELDS... HURRY UP, JENKINS!

2 OK, this is the bit that you've been waiting for. Flick the switch and turn on your power supply.

3 The power surge makes the atoms in the ruby wobble violently. They give out photons of red light. These bump into more atoms which wobble and make more photons.

4 A growing crowd of photons charges up and down the inside of the box reflecting off the mirrors. Eventually the light is so bright the photons actually flash *through* the mirror as a blinding beam of light.

5 All this power makes your ruby very hot. If your machine shows signs of over-heating simply chuck the water over it. (Some lasers have built-in water cooling systems.)

EXCITED PHOTONS

EXCITED SCIENTIST

Step 3 – how to shoot down missiles.

1 Simply get your plane in the air and keep an eye out for incoming missiles. You can use your heat detecting system to track the heat blasting from behind the enemy missile.

2 When you spot a missile aim the laser at its fuel tank. Try to keep the beam steady for a few seconds. The laser's heat will melt the missile's side and set fire to its fuel. The enemy missile will then blow up in mid-air and you'll have saved your school.

EXCELLENT JENKINS. I'LL MAKE SURE YOU GET A GOOD REPORT THIS TERM.

MAKING LIGHT WORK

Of course, your laser can do much more than zap enemy missiles. In fact, lasers can make light work of many jobs...

1 A laser beam makes a snappy-snipper! Lasers are used in factories to cut fabric at 15 m a second.

2 Laser beams read bar codes in shops or libraries. Take a look on the back of this book. Can you see a square with a pattern of lines? The pattern is a unique code for *Frightening Light*. If you bought the book you may have seen the shop assistant passing a scanner across the lines. A laser beam in the scanner flickers as it picks up the lines and the flickering beam is read by a computer that recognizes the code from the pattern of flickers. Here's an idea that's really on the right lines.

3 Lasers can be life-savers. They can cut through human flesh and heat seal the edges of a wound so you don't get bleeding. By firing a laser down an endoscope (that's a tube containing optical fibres, remember) you can perform life-saving operations deep within the body. A laser can even weld back a retina that has come adrift from the inside of the eyeball.

YOUR EYESIGHT WILL BE FINE AFTER THIS OPERATION, MR JENKINS

'WELD' DONE, DOC!

4 A laser beam "reads" a CD by flickering as it reflects off a pattern of pits on its surface. The CD player turns this flickering light signal into electric pulses and then into your fave pop music.

EDGE OF COMPACT DISC OR 'CD'

ERK! GREASY THUMB PRINTS RUIN CDS

CROSS SECTION OF CD

PIT

CD LASER

PULSES TRAVEL TO A CONVERTER

5 Laser beams travel in straight lines so you can use them to build nice straight tunnels. Simply fire a beam from the entrance of the tunnel and get digging along the line of the beam.

6 A laser beam can melt and weld metals. And unlike any other tool a laser beam never gets blunt with use.

7 Laser beams liven up pop concerts. Simply fire the laser into the air and wave it around to make dramatic light patterns. And then who cares if the music's rubbish?

8 Lasers can measure tiny earthquakes. Lasers on the San Andreas Fault, California are linked up to monitoring equipment. Any wobble in the light beam caused by a tremor in the ground can be instantly detected.

9 Laser printers work by firing an image of the page you're printing on to a light-sensitive drum. This drum has an electrical force which then picks up toner (the black stuff) and prints on to the paper. And laser printers are fast – maybe that's because they keep in toner – ha ha.

But that's just the start of what lasers can do ... they're so useful that scientists have really taken a shine to them, ha, ha.

Bet you never knew!
You can make holograms with lasers. All you have to do is...

BEAM SPLITTER   MIRROR

LENS

LENS

MIRROR   HOLOGRAPHIC
PLATE

Split a laser beam into two beams using a mirror. Fire one of these at an object. Make sure it then reflects on to a photographic plate. The other beam fires directly at the plate. When seen in daylight these dots form a 3-D pattern. Nowadays holograms appear on credit cards to stop crooks from copying them. So this discovery reflects to your credit!

SPEEDY SIGNALS

Don't forget light is *FAST* with a capital F. And so is laser light.

• In 0.14 seconds you can send a laser signal around the world.

• In 2.5 seconds you can send a light signal to the moon *and* back again. (In the 1960s US scientists did this. By timing the signal they were able to calculate the exact distance of the moon.)

• A laser could send a light signal to Mars in just three minutes. (The Martians' reply would take another three minutes.)

But laser signals aren't just for chatting with aliens. You probably use them to natter to your friends. Yes – every time you pick up a phone.

LISTENING LASERS

When you talk into a phone connected to an optical fibre cable the same technology that turns a laser light into sound in a CD works in reverse.

ELECTRIC PULSES ARE CONVERTED INTO LIGHT PULSES

LIGHT PULSES BOUNCE OFF THE FIBRE'S INSIDE SURFACE UNTIL IT REACHES THE OTHER END

OUR VOICES ARE CONVERTED INTO LIGHT SIGNALS, MILDRED!

ONE FIBRE OPTIC CABLE CAN HOLD THOUSANDS OF FIBRES

LIGHT PULSES ARE CONVERTED BACK INTO ELECTRIC PULSES

YOU DO TALK NONSENSE, BETTY. THAT WOULD NEVER WORK!

A microphone turns the sound of your voice into electric pulses which are transformed into laser light signals. These whiz down the cable.

At the other end of the line the process is reversed and you hear sounds in your earhole.

And because light moves so fast and a laser can flicker at billions of times a second an optical fibre can carry a conversation down the line in the blink of an eye. And what's more, you can squash thousands of fibres in a single cable.

And yet the wonders of optical fibres look pale compared with future developments. But is the future bright with promise or is it dark and frightening? Let's gaze into the crystal ball...

A BRIGHTER FUTURE?

Imagine there was no light on planet Earth except for your pocket torch. People would grope their way through the darkness to marvel at this amazing brightness. They would wonder at its beauty and its ability to turn darkness into colours and shadows.

But light is everywhere. And because we see it every day we don't think too much about it. What a pity.

Light is awesome, unbelievable, fantastic. And although the science of light seems frightening at first – the more you discover the more magical it seems. It's incredible that a humble light bulb makes photons and that these astonishing blips of energy can light up the sky in the day and at night you can see stars because their photons have travelled for millions of years to reach you.

It's even more astonishing to think that it's photons that give colour to a daffodil or power to a laser. And it's gobsmacking to peer in a mirror and know that you can only see yourself because every second billions of photons are bouncing off the mirror to create an image made of light.

But the latest discoveries of physicists are even MORE exciting, even more brain-boggling. And they're about to light up our future in totally unexpected ways. For example...

1 CREATIVE CHEMICAL CHAOS

In the 2000's scientists learnt how to use lasers to trigger chemical reactions. Traditionally, you had to heat things up over a grotty old Bunsen burner like the sort you find in schools.

But by using laser pulses of exactly the right length scientists can break chemicals into smaller groups of atoms to create brand new chemicals. And this could turn every industry that uses chemical reactions upside down.

2 SMALL IS BEAUTIFUL

Nowadays people can make a fibre optic cable thousands of times finer than the eye of a needle. And tiny lasers are possible too. In 1989 IBM made a laser one-tenth the thickness of a human hair. With a bit of careful packing you could fit a *million* of them into this box.

The laser was made from tiny crystals and this technology will make possible micro-holograms and tiny surgical instruments for delicate operations. In fact, miniature versions of any machine that uses a laser.

3 MARVELS IN STORE

By the 2000's, scientists had figured out how to stop and store light. At first this involved cooling atoms to ultra-cold temperature and trapping photons with lasers and magnets. But in 2005 scientists found that a purple substance made by slimy microbes could slow light too.

4 STRANGE LIGHT SIGNALS

By the 2000's scientists were experimenting with a brain-boggling effect called quantum entanglement. If you make a pair of photons, they behave as if they're in contact, even when they're hundreds of kilometres apart. You could even use this pair of freaky photons to send coded signals. And just imagine – you could combine tiny lasers and light storage and secrete photon codes to create something that makes a super computer like something your baby brother plays with...

5 THE ULTIMATE DREAM MACHINE

I'm talking about a computer that does billions of sums at the speed of light using photons to send information. And scientists are dreaming of such a machine – a machine so powerful that it could do all your maths homework for the next ten years in one-millionth of a second. Now that's progress for you!

Sure, light is the fastest moving thing in the universe. But science is beginning to catch up. The future's looking horribly bright – and that's the brilliant truth!

FRIGHTENING LIGHT QUIZ

Now find out if you're a
Frightening Light expert!

Light up Your Life!

So, have you been switched on during this lightning journey through light? Are you a bright spark or still in the dark? Take this quick quiz and find out...

1 What are the two main ingredients of a rainbow?
a) Sunlight and a pot of gold
b) Sunlight and rain
c) Sunlight and oxygen

2 What mysteriously occurs when a photon hits an atom?
a) All its energy is absorbed and, exhausted, it disappears
b) It has so much energy that it splits the atom into a million pieces
c) The photon's energy can glue atoms together

3 How long does it take speedy sunlight to reach the Earth?
a) About the time it takes for you to sneeze and wipe the snot on your sleeve during your Science lesson (8.5 seconds)
b) About the time it takes for you to nod off in your Science lesson (8.5 minutes)
c) About the time it takes for you to zoom out of the door at the end of your Science lesson (8.5 milliseconds)

4 How many light waves could stretch across the dot at the bottom of this question mark?
a) Hundreds

b) 4,677 precisely

c) About five

5 Which of the following would make an atom spit out a photon?

a) Asking it nicely

b) Sticking it in the freezer

c) Popping it in the oven

6 What happens to a stream of light when it moves from air into water?

a) It bends, or refracts

b) It bounces back, or reflects

c) It starts doing backstroke

7 Why is the sky blue?

a) Because there are more blue light waves than there are other colours

b) Because more blue light photons are scattered by the air

c) Because light is reflected off the water that covers 70 per cent of the Earth's surface

8 If a plant reflects green light and absorbs all the other colours, what colour light does a banana reflect?

a) Yellow

b) All colours except yellow

c) Red and green

Answers
1b; 2a; 3b; 4a; 5c; 6a; 7b; 8c

Meet the Scientists...

We'd still be living in the dark ages when it comes to light if it wasn't for a few freaky physicists who looked at light in a different way (often nearly blinding themselves in the process!). Can you match the discoveries below with the spectacular scientists responsible?

1 This freaky English physicist used a triangular lump of glass to prove that sunlight was made up of lots of different colours.

2 This German genius suggested that light came in the form of packets that he gave the curious name of 'quanta'.

3 This Dutch daredevil shed light on the mysteries of space by inventing the telescope.

BEAM ME UP, SCOTTY!

4 This mad-haired German-born scientist befuddled everyone by proving that light is both a wave and a particle (eh?!).

5 This ingenious American inventor set the world alight with his light bulb.

6 This famous French physicist found a way of measuring the speed of light using a spinning wheel and a mirror!

7 This amazing Arab scientist discovered that light is given out by glowing objects and that it always reflects at a predictable angle.

8 This energetic Englishman wowed the world with his discovery that light travels in weird waves.

a) Thomas Young
b) Armand Fizeau
c) Thomas Edison
d) Isaac Newton
e) Ibn al-Haytham
f) Hans Lippershay
g) Max Planck
h) Albert Einstein

Answers
1d; 2g; 3f; 4h; 5c; 6b 7e; 8a

What Does It All Mean?

These strange scientists used many weird and wonderful words to describe the ways light behaves and the objects it interacts with. Look at the list of words below – can you remember what on Earth they all mean?

1 Transparent
2 Reflection
3 Frequency
4 Interference
5 Refraction
6 Opaque
7 Diffraction
8 Translucent

a) The bizarre bending of light as it passes from one material to another.
b) The strange spreading out of light waves after they've passed through a small slit.
c) The name for an object that can block light and cast a spooky shadow.

d) The name for a frosty object that isn't so solid no

light can get through … but isn't completely see-through, either.

e) The bouncing back of light when it hits an object.

f) The name for something that has a thin layer of regularly spaced atoms which means lots of light can pass through.

g) The mysterious meeting of light waves when they make a brighter light or block each other out completely.

h) The number of times a weird wave of light wiggles each second.

Answers
1f; 2e; 3h; 4g; 5a; 6c; 7b; 8d

Light Fantastic

Light is so amazing that you simply won't believe some of the things people say about it. Have a look at these fantastical statements and see if you can figure out which are strange but true and which are just strange…

1 You are only able to see your annoying little brother because light waves are bouncing off him.

2 Light is so brilliant it can even bend around corners.

3 Sunlight is made up of seven colours – red, orange, yellow, green, blue, indigo and violet.

4 Eating carrots helps you to see in the dark.

5 All the light on Earth comes from the sun – without our super star we'd all die in the darkness.

6 Stars seem to twinkle because the light from them is being bent by eerie gusts of wind.

7 People who are colour blind only see things in black and white.

8 Light is faster than anything, anywhere, ever…

Answers

1 TRUE. You'd probably rather be left in the dark…

2 TRUE (AND FALSE). Ha ha! Trick question. Light waves can only travel in straight lines, but amazing scientists have invented things called optical fibres that can carry light round corners.

3 FALSE. Sunlight is made up of these seven colours and everything in between (and others on either side, actually). It's just that we only have specific words to describe seven of them.

4 FALSE. That's just a load of carroty cobblers. If you want to see in the dark, use a torch!

5 FALSE. Light can come from lots of other things – candles, your toaster, even curious creatures like fireflies. But we'd still all die if the sun stopped shining because sunlight is what helps plants grow, which keep us alive (but that's a whole other Horrible Science book…).

6 TRUE. Starlight moves in a straight line, like all other light, but it can be refracted by wild winds.

7 FALSE. People who are colour blind can usually distinguish some colours but not others.

8 TRUE. Nothing in the whole universe can travel faster than light.

Awesome Eyesight

Without your amazing eyes you'd be completely in the dark. These miraculous machines take in light, figure out colours and form an image in your brain. So, let the light waves bounce off the page and use the clues to answer these curious questions about sight.

1 Which bit of your bulging eyeball lets in light? (CLUE: It may be the class swot)

2 What's the matter with you if you have mysterious myopia? (CLUE: You'll have to look closely to answer this one)

3 What happens to an object if you look at it through a concave lens? (CLUE: This is just a tiny clue)

4 What happens to your peculiar pupils when it gets dark? (CLUE: Oh – open your eyes!)

5 Which part of your awesome eye bends the light so you see things in focus? (CLUE: It sounds corny, but it's true)

6 If an object reflects all types of light, what colour do your eyes see it as? (CLUE: You know the answer, all white)

7 Which little bits on your retina allow you to see things in glorious Technicolour? (CLUE: You wouldn't want to put you ice cream in them, though)

8 What kind of lens makes an object look bigger? (CLUE: It's not complex)

Answers
1 The pupil
2 You are short-sighted
3 It looks smaller
4 They get bigger to let in more light
5 The cornea
6 White
7 Cones
8 Convex

GULP!

HORRIBLE INDEX

accommodation (focuses light) 50–1

after-images 135

Alpha Centauri (our starry neighbour) 69

Andromeda galaxy, far, far away 69

angles of reflection 101

angles of refraction 120

arc-lights, dangerous 78–9

Archimedes (Greek scientist) 93

argon (gas) 88

astigmatism (eye problem) 116

astronomers, artful 21, 23–4, 26, 35, 62, 69–72, 90, 120

atoms, amazing 6, 15, 18, 20, 57, 71, 77, 79–80, 92, 98, 105, 108, 112, 124, 129–31, 137, 139–40, 144, 153–4

Ayrton, W.E. (British physicist) 96

bacteria, billions of 71, 74

bananas 126

bar codes 145

Basov, Nikolai (Russian scientist) 142

beeswax 78

Bell, Alexander Graham (American inventor) 141

binoculars 115

bioluminescence, brilliant 71

black 123, 127, 133–5

black holes 90–1

blindness 6, 54, 61, 79, 90

blood, black 127

bloodshot eyes 45

blue 6, 126, 128–35, 137–9

bottoms, glowing 75

Bradley, James (British astronomer) 26

brains, busy 40–1, 132, 135

Brocken Mountain, ghosts on 8, 10, 66

Bunsen burners, blasted 153

cameras 115

candles 10, 33, 77–8

canes, cruel 39

carbon dioxide (gas) 57

carbon filaments, in light bulbs 83, 86–7

cataracts (fluid in lens) 55, 61

cats 11, 134

CDs 146, 150

cells (body blobs) 42–4, 48, 61, 70, 74, 91, 134–5, 139

chemistry, chaotic 33, 45, 153

chromatic aberration (telescopic problem) 119–20

ciliary muscles (eyeball bits) 42, 51

clouds 90–1

codes 145, 154

coins, disappearing 110–11

colour deficiency 137–9

colours, crucial 13, 18, 30–2, 36–7, 44–5, 69–70, 112, 120–39, 152

comb jellies (glowing creatures) 74

computers 144–5, 154–5

concave lenses/mirrors (curve inwards) 102, 113, 115, 118, 120
concerts 147
cone cells (eyeball bits) 42, 44, 48, 134–5, 139
contact lenses 6, 118
convex lenses/mirrors (curve outwards) 103, 113–14, 116–17, 119
Coolidge, William (American inventor) 88
copepods (luminous plankton) 75
cornea (eyeball bit) 43–4, 49–51, 113, 116
credit cards 148
cross-eyed people, uncoordinated 45
crying 43, 52
crystals 91, 96, 154

Dalton, John (British chemist) 137–8
Davy, Humphrey (British scientist) 78
De la Rue, Warren (British photographer) 62–6
deep sea angler fish (glowing fish) 74
defence systems 143
deserts, dry 110
diffraction (light waves spreading out) 37
dinoflagellates (luminous plants) 75

earthquakes, measuring 147
eclipses, eerie 58–66
Edison, Thomas (American inventor) 80–7
Egyptians, awesome 93
Einstein, Albert (German scientist) 22, 38–41
Einstein, Hans (son of Albert) 40
Einstein, Mileva (wife of Albert/mathematician) 40

electricity 22, 78–81, 83, 85, 88, 112, 146, 148, 150
electromagnetism 6, 18
electrons, energetic 18, 80
endoscopes (look inside bodies) 91, 146
experiments, exciting 19–22, 27, 32, 35–6, 38, 45–6, 60–1, 67–9, 79, 98, 100–6, 110–11, 125, 134–7
expulsion 39
eyeballs, bulging 6, 23, 41–55, 90–1, 101, 114–18, 120, 126, 129, 134–9, 146
eyebrows 98
eyelashes 43

fact files, frightening 10, 92, 107, 123
factories 145
Fick, Adolf (German inventor) 118
films, for cameras 132
filters 132
fire flies (glowing beetles) 75
fish tanks, light-bending 107–8
Fizeau, Armand (French physicist) 26–7
flares, fiery 63, 66
fluorescent lights, flickering 80
focus 49, 51–2, 113, 116–18, 120–1
forces, fatal 22, 27
frequency (energy levels) 18, 123
Fresnel, Augustin Jean (French physicist) 37
future trends 152–5

galaxies, great 69
Galileo Galilei (Italian scientist) 24–6
gamma rays, deadly 18
gaslight 79
germs, gruesome 76, 136
ghosts, no such thing as 6, 8–10, 66, 104–5, 112, 141
glasses, wearing 115–18
glaucoma (gloop in eyeball) 54

glow, ghastly 10, 71, 73–7
glow-worms (beetles) 75
goggles 61, 91
Gould, Gordon (American scientist) 142
gravity, groovy 27
green 123, 126, 132–5, 138–9

halos 53, 120–1
heat 10, 13, 18, 22, 38, 78–9, 81, 94, 145
Herschel, John (British astronomer) 62–6
historians, horrible 100
holograms 148, 154
Hooke, Robert (British scientist) 32–4
horizon, horizontal 110
hospitals 23
Huygens, Christiaan (Dutch astronomer) 35, 37
hyperopia (long-sightedness) 116

Ibn al-Haytham, Abu al-Hassan (Arab scientist) 98–101
illusions, illusory 46
infections, unnecessary 136–7
interference (meeting of light waves) 37
Invisible Man 112–13, 124
iris (eyeball bit) 42, 54

Jannsen, Zacharius (Dutch inventor) 118

keratometers (eyeball-curve measurers) 118
Kruesli, John (Edison's assistant) 82

Langmuir, Irving (American inventor) 88
lasers, blistering 6, 27, 139–52, 154

Leavitt, Henrietta (American astronomer) 70
legs, short and stumpy 109
lenses, in eyeballs 43, 45, 48–9, 51, 55
lenses, made of glass 113–20, 148
Liebig, Justus von (German chemist) 94
light bulbs, brilliant 5, 11, 18, 56, 77, 80–9, 152
light waves 5, 14–15, 18, 35–8, 123
lighthouses 79, 88
Lindsay, James Bowman (Scottish inventor) 87
Lippershey, Hans (Dutch inventor) 118–19
long-sighted people 116–17
luciferin (glowing chemical) 71

Mackenzie, J.V. (Edison's assistant) 82–3
magnification 14, 114
Maiman, Theodore (American physicist) 142
matter, made of 15
Maxwell, James Clerk (Scottish physicist) 132, 138
mercury, uses for 79–80, 94
methane (gas) 76
Michelson, Albert (American scientist) 27
microbes, slimy 154
microscopes 14, 34, 107, 115, 118
mirages 90–1, 110
mirrors, murderous 12–13, 17, 26–7, 61, 89–91, 93–6, 98, 102–6, 113, 120–1, 143–4, 148, 152–3
missiles, shooting down 143, 145
mixing colours 132–4
moon, magic 12–13, 16, 58–60, 63–6, 71, 149
Murdock, William (Scottish inventor) 79
music 32, 146–7
myopia (short-sightedness) 116

Newton, Isaac (British scientist) 22, 27–34, 37, 120–1, 135–7
Nicholas of Cusa (German churchman) 117
Nichols prisms 130
Nobel Prizes 131, 142
nuclear explosions 55

observatories 23
ophthalmologists (eyeball doctors) 23, 50, 116
ophthalmoscopes (look at eyeballs) 91
optic nerves (eyeball bits) 42, 54
optical fibres 91–2, 146, 150–1, 154
optical physicists (light scientists) 22
opticians (eyeball testers) 118
optics 22, 100–1
oxygen (gas) 44, 71, 76

paraffin candles, hazardous 78
patents 86, 142
Perry, J. (British physicist) 96
phones 149–51
phonographs (record players) 81
phosphor/phosphorus (glowing chemical) 77, 80
photography 132–3
photons, frightening 6, 14–18, 20–1, 24, 38, 45, 48, 57, 61, 69–70, 77, 80, 92–3, 98, 108, 129–31, 141, 143–4, 152–5
physicists, forceful 22, 37–8, 96, 142, 153
pigments (colour chemicals) 45, 112–13, 124
plague, bubonic 29, 33
Planck, Max (German physicist) 37–8
plankton, luminous 75
printers 148
prisms, pesky 28, 30–3, 121, 130
Prokhorov, Alexander (Russian scientist) 142
pupils (eyeball bits) 44, 47, 49

quanta (energy blips) 37–8
quantum electrodynamics (photon-swaps) 98
quantum entanglement, spooky 154

radio waves 18, 140–1
rainbows, ravishing 12–13, 30–2, 123
Raman, Chandrasejhara Vankata (Indian scientist) 127–31
random deviation 6
rattlesnakes, poisonous 12–13
red 18, 32, 124–7, 130, 132–5, 137–9, 144
reflections (bouncing light) 13, 20, 23, 37, 47, 61, 89–106, 111, 118, 121, 123, 125–7, 129–31, 133, 144, 146
refraction (bending light) 21, 31, 37, 45, 49, 51, 55, 71, 91, 107–13, 120, 135
relativity theories, revolutionary 38
retina (eyeball bit) 42, 44–5, 113, 116–18, 120, 134–5, 138, 146
road signs 90–1
rods (eyeball bits) 42, 44, 48, 50–1, 53–4, 61, 70
Roemer, Ole (Danish astronomer) 26
Romans, rotten 93
Royal Society (top science club) 32

scanners 145
Schawlow, Arthur (American scientist) 141
scientists, bright 5, 21–41, 48–9, 76, 80, 91, 93, 95–6, 98–101, 103, 113, 127–30, 134–8, 140, 142, 148–9, 151, 154–5
sclera (eyeball bit) 43

scrying (fortune-telling) 96
sea 128–31
Secchi, Angelo (Spanish scientist) 66
seeing double 54–5
shadows, sinister 10, 58, 61, 64, 66–8, 85, 125, 152
sheepskin, glowing 80
shellfish 90–1
shoes, shiny 97
short-sighted people 116–18
signals, speedy 149–50, 154
sky 6, 11, 110, 128–31, 152
snow blindness 90–1
sodium, uses for 79, 127
space 38
spectres 10, 66
spectroscopes (colour-studying instruments) 121
speed of light 22, 24–7, 108, 155
spiders, hairy 114–15
squid 134
staring, dangers of 61
stars, super 11, 23, 42, 56–7, 60, 64, 69–71, 152
street lights 79, 127
strip lights 80
Strutt, John (British scientist) 127–30
Strutt, Robert (John's son) 130–1
sun, swallowed 59–60, 64–6
sunlight/sunshine, sizzling 5, 10–13, 30–2, 55–72
sunsets 122, 129
Swan, Joseph (British inventor) 80, 86–7
swimming pools, light-bending 108–9

tallow candles, stinking 78
telescopes, traditional 26, 34, 107, 115, 118–20
television 90–1, 151
Thucydides (Greek writer) 59
time 38

toasters 18
toilets, glowing 75
tomatoes, tasty 124–5
toothpicks, in eyes 136
Townes, Charles (American scientist) 140–1
transparent (see-through) **things** 124
tungsten filaments 88

ultraviolet light 18, 80
university laboratories 22

Venetians, top secret 94
violet 18, 134, 138
vision 134–9

wavelengths, wiggly 6, 121
welding 146
Wells, H.G. (British writer) 113
white light 123–4, 133, 135
whites of eyes 45
wicks, wicked 78
will o' the wisps 76

X-ray fish 124

yellow 126, 134–5
Young, Thomas (British scientist) 34–7, 48, 138

171

HORRIBLE SCIENCE

Make sure you've got the whole horrible lot!

ISBN 978 0439 94449 6

EVERY BODY
NEEDS THEM!

HORRIBLE SCIENCE

BLOOD,
BONES and
BODY BITS

illustrated by
NICK ARNOLD   TONY DE SAULLES